Blessed Excess

SUNY Series in
Rhetoric and Theology

David Tracy and Stephen H. Webb, Editors

Blessed Excess

Religion
and the
Hyperbolic
Imagination

Stephen H. Webb

State University of New York Press

Production by Ruth Fisher
Marketing by Theresa A. Swierzowski

Published by
State University of New York Press, Albany

© 1993   State University of New York

For information, address State University of New York
Press, State University Plaza, Albany, NY 12246

Library of Congress Cataloging-in-Publication Data

Webb, Stephen H., 1961–
    Blessed excess : religion and the hyperbolic imagination / Stephen
H. Webb.
        p.   cm. — (SUNY series in rhetoric and theology)
    Includes bibliographical references and index.
    ISBN 0–7914–1357–8 (alk. paper). — ISBN 0–7914–1358–6 (pbk. :
alk. paper)
    1. Religion. 2. Hyperbole. I. Title. II. Series.
BL48.W313 1993
200'.14—dc20
                                                                    92–6298
                                                                    CIP

10 9 8 7 6 5 4 3 2 1

Christianity wants to destroy, shatter, stun, intoxicate: there is only one thing it does not want: *moderation*, and for this reason, it is in its deepest meaning barbaric, Asiatic, ignoble, un-Greek.

—Friedrich Nietzsche,
Human, All Too Human

A *little* exuberance is to be rejected as altogether unlovely.

—Søren Kierkegaard,
The Crisis and a Crisis in the Life of an Actress

Contents

Acknowledgments

In many ways, this project is a continuation of my first book, *Re-Figuring Theology, The Rhetoric of Karl Barth* (Albany: SUNY Press, 1991), where I approached Barth through a theory of tropes, focusing on metaphor, irony, and hyperbole. Although this work is more single-minded than its predecessor, it does develop the programmatic and no doubt enigmatic comments about hyperbole and rhetoric with which my first book concluded. It also expands and alters the theory of hyperbole that I articulated in chapter 4 of that book. In the interest of brevity alone, then, I have resisted naming many of the people whom I thanked in my book on Barth.

Several people have been significantly helpful in making this work possible. Dave Burgess, Ralph Chacon, Erik Parens, Raymond Williams, David Blix, Steve Smith, Peter Browning, Tom Stokes and Ken Chase have contributed general ideas and particular suggestions. Both Andy Laue and Dan Clark have taught me much—in personal and practical ways—about the promise and the peril of excess. Diane Timmerman, my wife, has been a close and constructive reader of these pages as well as a source of inspiration and encouragement. Finally, David Tracy of the University of Chicago Divinity School and William C. Placher of Wabash College have read all of these pages and have offered much direction to a project that easily could have careened out of control. David and Bill have been exceptional teachers and friends. Much of my theological education with them has helped to establish continuities and construct retrievals in my life where disruptions and lacunae existed before. From David I critically recovered the wonder of excess from my earliest spiritual experiences, the extravagant side of religion, so dangerous and yet so liberating, that theology too often neglects. From Bill I relearned—in opposition to the orthodox tenets of the academy—the importance of tradition and community, of letting language from the past shape, inform, and create the religious impulse. David keeps my imagination stretching, and Bill keeps refreshing it with the simple yet demanding stories and sayings of Christianity. To both of them this book is gratefully dedicated.

Introduction

———

Re-Figuring Religion:
Toward a Hyperbolic Imagination

———

We owe to Christianity, to the philosophers, poets, and musicians, a superabundance of deeply agitated feelings; to keep these from engulfing us, we must conjure up the spirit of science, which makes us somewhat colder and more skeptical, on the whole, and cools down particularly the hot flow of belief in ultimate truths, which Christianity, especially, has made so wild.
—Friedrich Nietzsche, *Human, All Too Human*

For we which now behold these present days
Have eyes to wonder, but lack tongues to praise.
—Shakespeare, Sonnet 106

My reflections begin with two interrelated questions. What would life be without excess, extravagant actions, extreme claims and visions—without, in a word, hyperbole? This question arises from the suspicion that contemporary discourse is becoming always more rational, more moderate, leveled flat by the contours of an unimaginative climate. The overwhelming success (defined in its own terms) and dominance of instrumental or technical rationality, the compulsive and relentless adjudicating of means and ends, leaves little room for other modes of discourse and praxis. Excess becomes defined as a temporary release from the tensive work—describing, explaining, ordering—that language *normally* is meant to accomplish. Hyperbole is an occasional eruption that soon subsides in order to make room for language as labor. When hyperbole is given a voice of its own, it is *used* in an efficient manner. Polemic—note for example the politicized debates currently polarizing the academy—is the one acceptable expression of hyperbole today, a form of attack that disguises itself with feigned sincerity and does not favorably compare to hyperboles that poetically extend myopic perceptions instead of insidiously negating an opponent.

The second question concerns religion: Is it not the role of religion, as well as art, to speak in excess, to break the bondage of everyday caution, to be hyperbolic? This question too arises from a suspicion. Religion has increasingly become commonplace because we have lost the sense of hyperbole which it once served. The only hyperbole religion seems to know is—like the wider culture—polemicized disputes and debates, to which religion often contributes a simplistic and inflammatory vocabulary that exaggerates divisions instead of enlarging visions. Outside of the unacknowledged configuration of polemic, we are unaware of how hyperbole might contribute to our deepest needs and concerns. At best, when we hear hyperbole at all today it sounds ridiculous, foolish, absurd, even fanatical. We are in danger of losing a dimension to language which stretches the imagination, challenges ready-made assumptions, and forces unusual perspectives.

Hyperbole and religion, I want to wager, are inextricably connected; their fates are interchangeable. Indeed, following the course of this trope in Western texts on rhetoric uncovers a social history as well as theories of style and persuasion. As religion has withered away in modern Western culture, so has hyperbole, and the demise of hyperbole goes pretty far in explaining the demise of religion. As the excessive claims of religion have been watered down by criticism and skepticism, only on the far right, in fundamentalism, has the connection between hyperbole and religion survived, frequently in a sinister form (and oddly connected to the literalism of science) which does neither hyperbole nor religion justice. Yet, the flourishing of fundamentalism is a sign that cannot be ignored; in such contentious clamor there is an unmistakable appeal that should serve as an admonition to all those who would keep religion closely guarded by reason and civility. To turn this warning into a question to those who seek the power of fundamentalism in an alternate form: Can we today learn again to imagine more than we know, say more than we dare to believe, act more boldly than we know is wise and rational, see more than realism displays, hope more broadly than the facts would allow? Can we again find the connection between religion and hyperbole—a hyperbolic imagination?

Connecting religion and hyperbole should not seem to be such a wild gesture. After all, the very term "religious" in ordinary parlance often means "excessive." When someone is warned not to hold a belief, any belief, so religiously, or when someone is accused of being religious about something, an extravagance is suggested that borders on unreason, an enthusiasm which threatens fanaticism. Religion today *is* superfluous, and the very word means superfluity. Many religious persons regret this fact, of course. Since the Enlightenment, the story goes, religion has moved away from the center of society and culture to the margins, and now religion is essentially problematic, forced into a defensive posture, inherently in need of explanation, subject to criticism and revision and more frequently rejection. Religion is a question, not an exclamation.

Perhaps this situation, the history of religion in the modern Western period, can be understood in a different light. I want to affirm that religion today is exaggeration, an excess that is a surplus, supererogatory, something that inefficiently exceeds the cautious boundaries of the utilitarian mentality, the rational, and the expected. The Enlightenment critique, therefore, has done a great service to religion, returning it to its proper sphere. For the-

ologians to work against this process of marginalization—and such work has constituted modern liberal theology since Friedrich Schleiermacher—is to force religion into a mold which it always overflows. Religion
cannot and should not be subjected to the demands of
the ordinary, the predictable, the usual. Religion
exceeds—and through hyperbole transfigures—the quo-
tidian imagination of modernity.

   Religion is exaggeration, but it is an exaggeration
that, to some people anyway, seems necessary, even
though there is no room for religion in the secular
world anymore. Precisely because there is no room for
religion it makes its own room, not by fitting into the
gaps of secular culture, diffusing the dogmatic constraints of modernity with a little mystery or morality,
but by requiring more, imagining more, and knowing
more than secular reality will permit. Religion pushes
above and beyond the ordinary limits of space and time
to disclose a supramundane dimension that does not
coincide with the here and now but nevertheless seems
more real than reality itself. Religion is nothing less
than that which is excessive, that which is, by definition, more than what can be known or felt, described or
contained. And yet, perhaps this excess itself fulfills a
need, satisfies a deficiency—stakes a claim to truth. Of
course, we know that we do not need religion anymore.
Nevertheless, we cannot settle for anything less. The
task of this book is to demonstrate the apparent—perhaps ironic?—oxymoron that religion is a necessary—a
blessed—excess, not useful, but also indispensable, a
mode of existence which, though claiming always more,
would forever diminish and impoverish the everyday
world were it ever to be dismissed as *mere exaggeration*.

   The first chapter establishes the theoretical structure and significance of hyperbole while applying that
trope to the simple claim, "God is love." Much recent
work in rhetoric has tried to argue that metaphor cannot simply be reduced to simile, to a comparison or

analogy. In this chapter I pay the same compliment to hyperbole: at its best, it is not mere emphasis or magnification; instead, its elevated language says something that could not be said in any other way. Just as metaphor creates a new image that is more than the comparative "like" of simile, hyperbole does not compare what is with what could be if it were only more; it says what is precisely by saying the more, and it claims that what is cannot be said in any other way. It claims that the "more" really "is." This understanding of hyperbole makes it especially suitable to an analysis of Christian love in the context of the problem of evil.

The subsequent chapters take the form of readings of various authors from this vantage point. While these chapters can be read separately, there is a theological line of reasoning at stake. Certain key theological moves, I suggest, are essentially related to the trope of hyperbole. Chapter 2 in fact continues the argument developed in chapter 1 by examining the rhetorical construction of love in the work of Søren Kierkegaard. Love puts into action the expansive force that hyperbole unleashes. I show that love, for Kierkegaard, is not only a kind of hyperbolic power; it is also hyperbolically construed. One can never love enough, just as one can never say enough about love. Love thus constitutes a transition point where tropology is translated into praxis.

Chapter 3 broadens my pursuit of hyperbole to encompass the simple but elusive category of excess—all those acts, gestures, and words that are more than the expected, the usual, and the normal. Perhaps no thinker has been more obsessed with excess than Georges Bataille. His deeply religious and yet atheistic interpretation of sacrifice as a form of extravagance, a nonproductive squandering that obeys no laws, is an attempt to liberate excess from all constraints, even from the machinations of religion from which it arises. Bataille pursues an excess that resides unspeakably beyond the border of language, an act of giving that dissolves the self in a disorienting silence. Nevertheless, his search does leave a trail of utterances, explanations, and improvisations, wagers for understanding. The problem is whether excess can ever be articulated outside of a framework of purposes, goals, and consequences. Indeed, Bataille's quest for a pure, absolute, antieconomical excess demonstrates the limitations of excess itself: excess is always an expression, combining desire and articulation, and therefore it demands placement in a wider arena that will, paradoxically, give it direction and value.

The next two chapters show how religious uses of excess can make sense of a trope that is essentially antisensical. Flannery O'Connor's hyperbolic construal of grace is the focus of chapter 4. Her fiction exhibits a subtle relationship between trope and theology. Instead of simply employing rhetoric for apologetical purposes, her excessive stories move toward mystery without guaranteeing any arrival. Hyperbole cannot deliver what it promises, no matter how far it can travel, but it can prod and poke the reader toward unusual visions and troubling transformations. O'Connor images dreams of excess that nightmarishly shatter any awakening return to reality, imposing on the reader the ontological question of what is really real. She pushes hyperbole toward its breaking point with only oblique suggestions about what lies beyond, in the aftermath of the ensuing explosion.

In the fifth chapter I further explore the limits of excess in that unabashed exaggerator, G. K. Chesterton. If O'Connor risks making too little sense, Chesterton risks making too much. Here the problem of hyperbole and meaning is sharply focused. Is hyperbole, that great liar of a trope, secretly reasonable? Is it coherent to suggest that some hyperboles make more sense than others? Does the nonsense of hyperbole ultimately make sense? Chesterton's purple prose is, I argue, closely guarded by an indefatigable faith in common sense that does not allow him to follow hyperbole very far. In the end, the pyrotechnics of his hyperbole fizzle into statements that go without saying because everybody already knows all about it; exaggeration, ironically, becomes understatement.

Chesterton belligerently raises, even if he does not satisfactorily answer, the fundamental question about hyperbole: Can one go all the way with hyperbole and still return with sound advice and reasonable opinions? Does hyperbole have a voice of its own? Does it have something to say that has not already been said and that cannot be said in any other way? Chapter 6 contrasts hyperbole with the current trope of choice, irony, claiming that something fundamental is lost when the manipulative desire to turn reality against itself is allowed to displace and overwhelm the basic need to see further than appearances alone permit. The last chapter also explores the relationship between hyperbole and prudence or moderation in order to show that excess is not a transient release from everyday constraints and restrictions but is a more permanent and necessary aspect of an imagination that extends and even breaks limits in order to return to a world more vividly fathomed. Finally, I play against Chesterton's inimitably sane insanity figures of excess, hyperbolic saints who make sense only through and not around their nonsense. Sometimes, I suggest, nonsense makes its own kind of sense: something more is just enough.

Throughout these chapters I argue that hyperbole has a varied, complex and essential role to play in religious discourse and praxis. Although I define, or better, describe hyperbole in chapter 1, its full range and implications arise only throughout the whole of this text; no single set of problems could exhaust its resourcefulness. However, a pattern does emerge in my treatment of this trope. I begin with a display of the rhetorical basis of the fundamental theological proposition that God is love. Then in chapter 2 I examine a classical encomium responsive to that proposition. I next show how excess can be driven to extremes of negativity in chapter 3 and positivity in chapter 5. Bataille and Chesterton, then, are two sides to the same problem, one pushing excess too far and the other not far enough. Between these two chapters I explicate a more subtle and therefore adequate treatment of what is an essentially disruptive phenomenon. Chapter 6 draws my thoughts together by contextualizing hyperbole in the broader tropical spectrum and placing it in a social and institutional setting.

Even though I acknowledge a pattern in my discussion of hyperbole, I still want to argue that this trope does not fit in any straightforward way into religious discourse. The category of hyperbole does not include all of religious language. In fact, much religious language is an attempt to discount and mitigate hyperbole. Indeed, hyperbole's own ambiguity helps to explain both the fascination and the repulsion many people feel toward religion. Without any simple shape or form, its power and persistence nevertheless go a long way toward figuring religious rhetoric. I have not tried to map all of its awesome peaks and troubling contours, but I have tried to follow this trope as far as I was able to go. My strategy, in brief, has been twofold. I have tried to provide a theory of hyperbole, in full recognition of the difficulty of developing an overview of that which signifies the highest, above which thought cannot transcend. I have also tried to reveal the structure and express the power of this trope by means of intensification and acceleration. I hope I will be understood if—in an attempt to correlate subject and style—I have occasionally followed hyperbole too closely by exaggerating its force and effectiveness.

Chapter
One

The (Il)Logic of Excess:
The Test Case of "God is Love"

My God, my God, thou art a direct God, may I not say a literal God, a God that wouldst be understood literally and
according to the plain sense of all that thou sayest? but
thou art also (Lord I intend it to thy glory, and let no profane misinterpreter abuse it to thy diminution), thou art a
figurative, a metaphorical God too; a God in whose words
there is such a height of figures, such voyages, such pere-
grinations to fetch remote and precious metaphors, such
extensions, such spreadings, such curtains of allegories,
such third heavens of hyperboles, so harmonious elocu-
tions, so retired and so reserved expressions, so com-
manding persuasions, so persuading commandments,
such sinews even in thy milk, and such things in thy
words, as all profane Authors seem of the seed of the serpent that creepes, thou art the Dove that flies.
    —John Donne, *Devotions Upon Emergent Occasions*

Nothing less than the infinite and the miraculous is necessary, and man does well not to be contented with anything less, and not to feel at home as long as he has not
acquired it.
    —Vincent Van Gogh, Letter to Theo

    In a now classic article, "Metaphor and Religion: The
Test Case of Christian Texts," David Tracy applies the
most recent theories of metaphor to both the parables of

Jesus and the Johannine claim that "God is love."[1] Borrowing from Stephen Pepper's notion of a root metaphor, Paul Tillich's method of correlating Christian claims with analyses of general human experience, and Paul Ricoeur's work on the hidden mechanism of metaphor, Tracy elaborates a systematic reading of the configuration of Christianity's most basic teaching. I want to broaden the rhetorical turn in theology to which Tracy has contributed so much by suggesting that this analysis could also be accomplished from the perspective of hyperbole. My argument should contribute both to a better understanding of hyperbole, a much neglected trope, and to the figural dimension of religious claims. Briefly stated, "God is love" is not merely the synthesis of two disparate discourses, the fusion typical of metaphor; it can also be understood as an excessive claim, made with the extravagant resources of hyperbole.

According to Tracy, a root metaphor provides the core around which a cluster or network of other images and arguments are sustained and organized. In religion, these centrally grounded branches of discourse sustain a fundamental claim about the need for and promise of salvation. "These networks describe the enigma and promise of the human situation and prescribe certain remedies for that situation" (89). The primary layer of religious meaning, then, does not reside with theological claims and contentions but with a poetic insight which is only indirectly articulated by the second-order language of theology. Tracy finds the clue to Christianity's poetic basis in the parables of Jesus. Drawing heavily from Paul Ricoeur, Tracy argues that the sayings which take the form of "The Kingdom of God is like..." are a conjunction of metaphor and narrative in which the logic of everyday language is suspended in order to bring together the extraordinary (the Kingdom of God) with the ordinary. In these portraits of the Kingdom, there is a clash between the realism of the narrative and the extravagance of its conclusions, and in this tension lies the power of metaphor.

A metaphor violates the usual logic of predication by identifying two subjects that normally lie far apart. The parables are extended metaphors: through a process of intensification, the ordinary is connected to the unexpected to make a distinctive and concrete image of what hitherto seemed impossible. Extravagant actions like a father's celebration of a returning prodigal son (to which I will return in the last chapter) or an employer's equal payment for workers hired late in the day serve—like all good metaphors—to disorient the reader. This initial shock is followed by a reorientation, which is the recognition that a new mode of being has been disclosed, a way of living based on the pure, unbounded love of God. The parables refer, then, to a Christian style of life based on fundamental trust and agapic love.

At the root of these parables is the simple message that takes the metaphoric form "God is love" (1 John 4:7). This statement is set in the genre of a letter, not the narrative of a parable, and thus it is part of a second-order conceptual and reflective discourse. Nevertheless, it is a metaphor that expresses the message of the parables in the most compact way. "God is love" contains a logic of superabundance that cannot easily be summarized or paraphrased. Tracy is aware, of course, that this metaphor does not convey the whole truth of Christianity. In fact, the metaphor engenders two kinds of interrogations, one based on love and the other on God. Theologians have long debated what love best expresses God's relationship toward us. Here questions about the interconnections among agape, eros, and caritas have been crucial. This metaphor, then, does not answer the question of what kind of love God is but rather serves as the basis for that question. Moreover, this metaphor cannot be isolated from other biblical images of God. It must be understood "in the context of the wide spectrum of alternative metaphors for 'God' employed in the Old and New Testaments: from king, shepherd, rock, lord to light, truth and wisdom" (102). Tracy even argues that the image of the wrath of God serves as an essential qualification to this metaphor; otherwise, God's love could easily be sentimentalized.

The important point is that "God is love" "is not simply a descriptive account of an observed empirical reality" (103), and thus, like any good metaphor, it cannot be reduced to conceptual clarification, although such clarification might be helpful. This metaphor provides a productive and tensive account of the relationship between a comparatively unknown (God) and a known (love), which creates an image whose surplus of meaning, though it cannot be replaced, can produce second-order discourse and debates. Theology does not replace but helps us to understand the religious meaning of this metaphor: religiously speaking, the metaphor both enables and commands Christians to love as they have been loved; the indicative entails and discloses an imperative.

Although Tracy uses the language of hyperbole throughout this text—excess and extravagance more than synthesis and fusion mark the statement "God is love"—he limits his tropical analysis to metaphor.[2] This is understandable: hyperbole is the poor relation of the tropes family, treated like a distant relative whose family ties are questionable at best. It is an illegitimate trope, rarely analyzed and utilized like metaphor or the equally popular trope of irony. After all, Aristotle argued that the effective use of metaphor is a sign of genius, but it is assumed that anyone can hyperbolize. Moreover, hyperbole is morally suspect because it is thought to be a sly and yet easily discernible attempt to say more than what the situation allows. In the *Nicomachean Ethics*, the earliest and still one of the most sustained and comprehensive attacks on excess ever written, Aristotle's connection of virtue and moderation leads him to condemn hyperbole as nothing more than deception.

To come to the point; in regard to truth, let us call the man in the middle position truthful and the

mean truthfulness. Pretense in the form of exaggeration is boastfulness and its possessor boastful,
while pretense in the form of understatement is self-
deprecation and its possessor a self-depreciator.[3]

Self control and tact not only define correct behavior
but also the pursuit of truth, in addition to the propriety of style.

Hyperbole is thus condemned both for its boldness
and its transparency, in other words, its immaturity.
Aristotle explains the prejudice: "Hyperboles are for
young men to use; they show vehemence of character"
(*Rhetoric*, 1413a29-30). As this quotation suggests,
hyperbole is often associated with polemical discourse
(diatribe and denunciation, a wanton disregard for caution and collegiality) as well as with childish talk (children probably learn it first among the tropes by being
warned against it). It is also associated with fanaticism
(a stubborn refusal to qualify or modify grandiose
statements) and insincere flattery. Recall, for example,
the beginning of *King Lear* in which Cordelia's sisters,
at the King's encouragement, exaggerate their love for
Lear while Cordelia, sickened by the deceit of this spectacle, chooses to understate her own feelings. This
unnatural trope breaks the boundary of the ordinary
decorum of language and so is mistrusted by definition.
Yet, as Lear understood but Cordelia refused to admit,
there is something attractive, even seductive about
exaggeration. Extreme claims, extravagant assertions,
excessive visions all have a power over us that is at
least as strong as our desire to deny it.

Even though this lesser trope is not considered as
dignified as metaphor, the rhetorical tradition has
given it sufficient treatment to establish a coherent pattern of approaches and analyses. One of the most moving and sustained discussions of hyperbole is contained in Longinus's *On the Sublime* (*Peri Hupsous*).[4]
Here elevated language is praised as an irresistible
power that articulates a noble passion and transports

the audience into transformative states of the imagination: "For I would make bold to say that nothing contributes to greatness as much as noble passion in the right place; it breathes the frenzied spirit of its inspiration upon the words and makes them, as it were, prophetic" (11). This apparent affirmation of extravagance is betrayed by the key phrase, "in the right place." Indeed, Longinus's own exaggerations of the wonders of the sublime ironically end in tight restrictions on this discourse. For Longinus, the sublime is an event in history, usually related to the heroic, which poetic language must try to capture or reflect.[5] Thus, sublime discourse cannot be indiscriminate; it must be measured by the reality which it is trying to describe. "To clothe petty matters in big and solemn words is like putting a big tragic mask on the face of an infant" (41).To invest the mundane with great emotion would be ridiculous, not sublime.

The transgression of hyperbole, then, is valid only if it recreates the emotions that are the due of great events. From Longinus's perspective, hyperbole should not attract attention to itself, but should modestly point to the experience which it conveys. Indeed, this conviction lies at the heart of Longinus's theory of poetry: "The best use of a figure is when the very fact that it is a figure goes unnoticed" (29). More specifically: "The best hyperboles are sometimes those which are not noticed to be hyperboles at all" (50). The most perfect art should be the most natural art; the condensation of experience into a pure form is the second nature of poetry, a nature that should be natural, transparent, allowing the audience to see through it to the sublime event itself. "For art at its best is mistaken for nature, and nature is successful when it contains hidden art" (33). The iconoclasm of hyperbole is redeemed by sacrificing itself to the subject matter, thus becoming incognito. An exaggeration named as such would be a failure.

The hyperbolist, by implication, must shape the exaggerated discourse to fit the experiences and expectations of the audience. "One must know, therefore, how far one can go in each case, for to go too far spoils the hyperbole's effect which, when overstrained, is weakened and may, on occasion, turn into its opposite" (49). Hyperbole should reproduce a shared event, conjuring emotions that are plausible and morally uplifting; if it is too shocking, too excessive, too unexpected, then it will alienate and provoke the audience, thus forsaking that unity of experience which is the precondition for the sublime. Nevertheless, Longinus is aware that excessive discourse is not so easily contained. "Great writing does not persuade," he admits, "it takes the reader out of himself...Greatness appears suddenly; like a thunderbolt it carries all before it and reveals the writer's full power in a flash" (4). However, Longinus eagerly laments the fact that it is too easy to go too far in trying to achieve startling effects; tawdriness and affectation are the result of hyperbole that does not aim at the proper objects and with the proper tone. Such excess, cunning and contrived, will appear artificial, selfishly detracting from the heroic situation and its moral message and focusing instead on itself, a style shorn of substance.

For the most part, the Greco-Roman tradition displays a unanimity on this trope, although it is not always as eloquently expressed as in Longinus. The *Ars poetica* of Horace, written between 23 and 13 B.C.E., reflects the common classical theme of prudence and appropriateness in speaking and writing, urging the avoidance of extremes in poetry. The poet should choose a theme equal to the poet's strength and should know how to say the right thing at the right time. New and strange words should be used only in moderation; words and actions should fit both the speaker or character and the audience's expectations. Although this treatise does not explicitly address hyperbole, it clearly leaves no place for the trope of excess in its warnings against transgressing the boundaries of the expected.

The pseudo-Ciceronian *Rhetorica ad Herennium*

provides the most explicit and influential Latin definition: "Hyperbole [*superlatio*] is a manner of speech exaggerating the truth, whether for the sake of magnifying or
minifying something."[6] On first view, this definition,
which couples hyperbole with understatement (litotes),
seems to align this trope with the truth. However, on a
closer reading it is clear that hyperbole does not create a
truth, but rather magnifies something that is already
true. Indeed, the author of this text also classifies
hyperbole as a form of emphasis (*significatio*) and notes
that metaphor too is used to magnify or minify. The
truth, then, is independent of the workings of this trope.

Hyperbole is thus portrayed as more like simile,
which points out a previously known similarity, than
metaphor, which creates new meaning through a unique
fusion of seemingly incompatible elements. Simile
works on the basis of resemblance, articulating a like-
ness which is already present for all to see; similarly,
hyperbole merely magnifies, calling attention to something that can be seen clearly without the occasionally
helpful aid of emphasis. This connection is unfortunate
for the history of hyperbole: an exaggeration of something already known would hardly be a remarkable figurative feat; instead, it would be a useful tool in some
situations but, if taken too far, it would become a nuisance, perhaps an irrelevant irritation, at best an amus-
ing diversion. I want to argue that the connection that
needs to be drawn is between hyperbole and metaphor,
not simile. Although poor hyperbole might function
like simile, good hyperbole does not emphasize the
truth but says something true through the exaggeration, a truth that could not be grasped in a nonfigural
form. Good hyperbole, like good metaphor, has a staying power that cannot be resisted with paraphrase and
summation. The excess of hyperbole is essential to the
truth that hyperbole speaks.

Quintilian (35 C.E. to sometime after 95) continues
and strengthens the Ciceronian attempt to connect
rhetoric and ethics in a plea for honesty and sincerity.

His extremely influential *De Institutione Oratoria* describes, in twelve books, the lifelong education of the orator. This education is a process which, without any hard rules, teaches public speaking as a way of life, and thus the book touches on many subjects in addition to rhetoric. When Quintilian writes about style, for instance, his concern is to establish the trustworthiness of the speaker, and so he emphasizes a natural and plain vividness that leaves no room for hyperbole. In fact, he laments the decline of Ciceronian moderation:

> Straightforward language, naturally expressed, seems to some of us to have nothing of genius; but whatever departs, in any way, from the common cause, we admire as something exquisite; as, with some persons, more regard is shown for figures that are distorted and in any respect monstrous, than for such as have lost none of the advantages of ordinary conformation.[7]

Indeed, echoing Aristotle's comment about the youthfulness of hyperbole's vehemence, Quintilian notes, "For clarity is the chief virtue of eloquence, and the less ability a man has, the more he tries to raise and swell himself out, as those of short stature exalt themselves on tiptoe, and the weak use most threats."[8] Distorting the common definition of figures of speech as compensations for deficiencies in language, Quintilian suggests that excess is quite literally a substitution for personal—physical and moral—faults and weaknesses.

When he was not so concerned about the moral integrity of his orator, Quintilian could offer a wonderful definition of hyperbole as "an elegant straining of the truth."[9] He could also write, in what is perhaps the most paradoxical definition of this trope, "It is enough to say that hyperbole lies, though without any intention to deceive."[10] This baffling statement surely says more than it intends; by displaying hyperbole's ambiguous relation to deception, it nudges—strains—toward the question of truth. It is possible that Quintilian knew, and was echoing, Seneca's *On Benefits*, which provides the most positive and constructive definition of hyperbole in the ancient world:

> We overstate some rules in order that in the end they may reach their true value...The set purpose of all hyperbole is to arrive at the truth by falsehood. And so when the poet [Virgil] said: "Whose witness shamed the snow, their speed the winds," he stated what could not possibly be true in order to give credence to all that could be true...Hyperbole never expects to attain all that it ventures, but asserts the incredible in order to arrive at the credible.[11]

Quintilian, however, must assert the priority of an ethics of moderation over Seneca's more straightforward concern with rhetorical truth. "For although every hyperbole involves the incredible, it must not go too far in this direction, which provides the easiest road to extravagant affectation."[12] Hyperbole is a dangerous and slippery slope in which one can slide upward into unrestrained and foolish passion and self-indulgence.

In theology, this cautious attitude toward excess has continued as an inheritance from the classical Greek and Latin rhetorical traditions, as is clear in Augustine's Ciceronian comments about preaching in *On Christian Doctrine*.[13] Here he warns against the use of the "grand style" for any prolonged length of time. The subdued manner is better for teaching, and even for praising and condemning the moderate manner is often better than the grand. Only when discourse is "forceful with emotions of the spirit" (150) is the grand style appropriate. Within the confines of theological reflection, however, such emotions are ordinarily out of place. Other theologians would concur. For example, Calvin once wrote, "But we do not read of anyone being blamed for drinking too deeply of the fountain of living water."[14] He means that it is impossible to exaggerate the significance of the Bible or to write too much or say too much about it. However, his own rather severely circumscribed prose, as opposed for example to Luther's often reckless style, is enough to show that Calvin did not take his own advice literally.

Mentioning Luther's name should suggest that many theologians, including Augustine himself, have not always followed Augustine's advice. Indeed, these brief remarks are not intended to survey the complex history of the relationship between hyperbole and theology. Excess has always been an integral part of religious language, especially, for example, in the language of the mystics, but also in such varying discourses as prayer, polemics, and hagiography, as well as ritualized practices like religious festivals. Paul Ramsey has drawn the contrast between Greek and Christian thought precisely at the boundary between moderation and excess. "Yet the Christian ideal of character," he writes, "is not the same as the Greek, 'In nothing too much, and something of everything'; Aristotle's ethic of the 'mean' not the same as Jesus' 'ethic of the extreme.'"[15] Ramsey argues that the one thing Aristotle is immoderate about is the pursuit of moderation, while Augustine's description of temperance restrains all impulses except one, "so that love might give itself entirely and *without restraint* to that which is loved... There can never be too much love for God, nor too little of the impulses which impede it."[16] An excessive love for God organizes and orders all of our other loves; by allowing for hyperbole in one place Augustine puts moderation in its proper place.

During the Enlightenment,[17] however, the current of Aristotelian reservations about extravagance that runs through much of theology settled into prejudices that became deeply embedded in popular as well as philosophical attitudes. Since the Enlightenment sets the stage for all modern theology, the effect for hyperbole was disastrous. As one historian explains, "'Enthusiasm' was a dirty word in the eighteenth century...Reasonable moderate people agreed that enthusiasm was a bad thing."[18] And another historian reinforces this view: "Civilized man, it was assumed, would be wise to adhere to his beliefs sedately and in a reasonable spirit...'Enthusiasm' was equated with fanaticism, and was everywhere suspect."[19] Indeed, the eighteenth-century French rhetorician Du Marsais (1676–1756) recommended that hyperboles be introduced with "so to speak" or "if one may say so," rhetorical precautions which discount this figure even before it is spoken.[20] Religion, after playing a significant role in a century and more of terrible strife, was put in its place. Everyone knew that the claims of religion could "get out of hand" and result in fanaticism. And yet, to say, "God is, so to speak, love," seems a high price to pay for the disciplining and correcting of the negative aspects of religious zeal.

The prolific and popular Joseph Priestley provides an excellent summation of Enlightenment attitudes toward hyperbole in *A Course of Lectures on Oratory and Criticism* (1777).[21] This text echoes, and sometimes simply repeats, many of the comments about excess and extravagance from classical authors. He defines hyperbole in terms of the same kind of transference that metaphor involves: "The advantage of using hyperbole is, that the idea of one object may be heightened and improved by ideas transferred from other objects, and associated with it" (241). Nevertheless, there is a crucial difference that sets hyperbole apart; it is a departure from the truth in which "the untruth lies in the affirmation itself, whereas in most other figures it is concealed in an epithet" (241). Thus, hyperbole's distortions are more direct and immodest than the other tropes.

Priestley does acknowledge that such directness can serve a useful function in discourse. To express really great magnitudes or numbers, hyperbole might be a necessary deception. However, hyperboles "must be condemned, as strained and unnatural, when the idea they excite in our minds really exceeds the idea that ought to be excited by the object described by them"

(243). When hyperbole goes further than the object that it represents, an object, of course, that Priestley admits it can never reach anyway, it has gone too far, and substitutes passions for the real thing. The expression should be molded by the idea of the object; it should not draw attention to itself as it tries to draw the reader or listener toward what cannot be literally understood. In the end, Priestley agrees, it is easy to abuse this trope, but not because of the nature of hyperbole itself but due to the tendency of human nature to deceive, "for what can be easier than to exceed the truth in description?" (244). The greedy logic of hyperbole is the shape of the desire to go further than the facts in the name of something else.

Contemporary writers are hardly more generous to the trope that lies. One of the most sustained and systematic treatments of hyperbole in recent literature can be found in the encyclopedic work by Chaim Perelman and L. Olbrechts-Tyteca, *The New Rhetoric.* These authors analyze this trope as an adjunct and subordinate to a specific type of argument, which they call "unlimited development," a structure or pattern of persuasion which insists "on the possibility of always going further in a certain direction without being able to foresee a limit to this direction, and this progress is accompanied by a continuous increase of value" (287). This argument protracts a line of thought that is already approved and valued, thus intending to define certain purified notions or promote unattainable ideals. Although they admit that there is an enormous margin of liberty in the creation of good hyperboles, they tend to limit it to this one particular argumentative strategy, the structure of which is clearly explained. They thus undervalue the reckless and profuse side to this trope.

An unlimited argument does not seek a certain destination, does not want to arrive anywhere; rather, it is driven by a telos always to go further, to say ever something more, to overstep itself. Such an argument is, by the very logic of *The New Rhetoric,* hardly an argument any longer. It does not seek to persuade by establishing some common ground; indeed, the metaphor of common ground is particularly inappropriate for a trope that seeks not just higher but even unimaginable terrain. Moreover, the authors of *The New Rhetoric* tend to limit hyperbole to the establishment of absolute or perfect terms. I see no warrant for this claim. Hyperbole can push in many different directions, toward the ideal and the ridiculous, the beautiful and the ugly, the acceptable and the unacceptable. This point will become particularly significant when I look at Flannery O'Connor.

Another important recent evaluation also follows this strategy of containment by connecting hyperbole to the search for the ideal, or the sublime. This connection has a long tradition, dating back to Longinus but also found in Samuel Johnson.[22] For Louis Wirth Marvick, the sublime is defined in terms of "the quality of an ideal which, despite [the artist's] best efforts, remains more or less aloof."[23] The language of the sublime is, therefore, both an exalting and bitter task; to speak about something that does not exist, or at best exists only ideally, something we desire but know we cannot obtain, is frustrating and demanding. Marvick argues that such language takes the form of hyperbole. Hyperbole not only believes in the sublime but also acts as an emotional discharge, channeling an enthusiasm that can become wild, fanatical, and dangerous. Indeed, Marvick suggests that hyperbole is intrinsically deceptive, passing off a lie "by injecting so heavy a dose of idealism into his [the reader's] fare, that the resistance of his faculties is overcome, and he gives himself up to the enjoyment of the illusion" (51). The metaphor here is illuminating: hyperbole is a numbing drug—an opiate for the masses?—that replaces one's sense of reality with a transitory hallucination.

According to Marvick, this deceptive strategy works, as in Longinus's analysis, only with the consent of the audience, without which hyperbole turns brutal

and ridiculous. Hyperbole is so passionate and naive
that only an audience desperately desiring to be
uplifted and overcome will submit to its frantic manipulations. Marvick has succeeded in portraying hyperbole as a part not of rhetoric but rather of psychology,
as a key to the phenomenon of mass hallucination and
irrational crowd behavior. Indeed, he argues that hyperbole must be cut with irony in order for it to seem palat-
able, let alone credible. I will focus on a more positive
relationship between hyperbole and the sublime in the
next chapter, where I will discuss Kierkegaard's notion
of love. Although I have learned much from Marvick, he
does leave unresolved the question of why anyone
would want to use this trope, or why anyone would be
fooled by it.

Indeed, the overwhelming verdict that rhetorical
tradition passes on hyperbole raises a suspicious question: What is this trope, that it engenders such consistent, even excessive criticism and rejection? Although
its wide scope and many manifestations will emerge
only throughout the various chapters in this book, I
want to try to better grasp, if not define, this trope in
the present chapter. The problem is that historically
hyperbole has rarely been given the honor of being
defined as a trope at all. When it is not being discussed—from the viewpoint of nature, order, and reason—in terms of compensation, deception, and passion, it is assigned, in rhetorical terminology, to the
second order of the tropes, along with such minor persuasive ploys as amplification, examples, and images.[24]
Hyperbole is thus not a trope in itself but an intensifier;
it can heighten any tropical gesture and so is dependent
upon other configurations. It has no definite shape of
its own but is felt when any trope goes too far. It
exhibits a supplementary logic, adding to other linguistic forms without making its own mark. A supplement,
however, is more than an addition; it also completes a
lack or corrects an omission.[25] Even more, a supplement reveals an incompletion, disclosing possibilities

that only a premature closure could preclude. Hyperbole is difficult to describe not only because it goes beyond ordinary discourse but also because it judges and indicts the ordinary from a vantage point that is always possible but rarely pursued.

Whatever it is, hyperbole always seems to invite prodigal speculation; a discussion of this figure of speech inevitably expands to include broader and larger issues. Perhaps this means that hyperbole's structure, the logic of a supplement that claims for itself a certain necessity and integrity, can never be precisely pinpointed. It is not accurate or fair, however, to infer from this ambiguity the conclusion that hyperbole is a secondary and derivative feat of the linguistic imagination. In fact, it could be argued that hyperbole constitutes the ultimate shape of all of the tropes. The desire to magnify, enlarge, and intensify is the basic drive of all tropical formations. Hyperbole is thus the primary trope, the Ur-trope, not an aspect of but on the contrary the root of all rhetoric. It is the master trope, the one mad movement that the other tropes imitate, shape, and even minimize in their own particular ways. I will return to the question of comparing tropes in the last chapter, but even given this positive understanding of hyperbole the question of a definition is still exceedingly difficult. After all, hyperbole is impossible to measure. Just how it extends beyond normal discourse is not very easy to determine: how far must the "too far" go in order to be considered hyperbolic? Moreover, because discussions of hyperbole tend to expand beyond the boundaries of rhetoric, any attempt at a definition is complicated by the fact that the reference of hyperbole is not limited to specific statements; instead, the term can also cover—as will be seen in the chapter on Georges Bataille—a broad range of meanings, namely, the hyperbolic: a force, an attitude or posture, any person or event or even thing that is disproportionate to the ordinary and everyday.[26]

For these reasons, it is best to begin simply. In very

practical terms, hyperbole seems to play a regular role in everyday discourse, and many hyperboles are easy to recognize. One of the most interesting facets of this trope is that it functions as both a species of language and action, and the interconnection between these two aspects is often not very clear. As a trope, hyperbole has been linked with "purple prose," a tendency toward flamboyance and extravagance, a willed excess that is often signified by an accumulation of words, proliferation of images, and extension of claims. As action, hyperbole breaks with the moderation that Aristotle found in all reasonable people by evincing an enthusiasm that the Enlightenment so thoroughly condemned. Hyperbole the trope is a strange feat of language, residing uneasily on the border of the sublime and the ridiculous; by going too far it can lose all sense of seriousness and purpose. Hyperbolic praxis can be located at the edge of an enthusiasm undefended against the temptation of fanaticism. In either case, as trope or praxis, hyperbole is usually suspect because, by definition, not only does it go too far but it is difficult, in the midst of good hyperboles, to say when the "too far" is "too much."

In fact, many definitions, like Perelman's and Marvick's, are limited not only because of their morally condemnatory (and condescending) tone, or because they connect hyperbole only to the ideal, an artificial constraint. These definitions fall short primarily because they make hyperbole an easy, transparent trope, an approach that does not account for its power and persistence. Hyperbole stubbornly insists that its violation of expectations be taken literally for good reason; as one writer explains, "Hyperbole is an exaggeration on the side of truth."[27] Indeed, hyperbole's literalness is its strength; because it aggressively wants to mean what it says, it cannot easily be reduced to a more tame equivalent. The more such power is taken seriously, the less definitions seem appropriate or even possible. To define is to limit, and in this arena of discourse only tentative boundaries can be constructed.

Among all the tropes, therefore, hyperbole is the most difficult to define because it is an inordinate movement and a violent impulsion—not a static formation or configuration—that breaks through ordinary limitations; hyperbole vertiginously suspends the logic of language, and therein lies the origin of its danger and power. A disruptive and visceral force, hyperbole cannot be measured because it opens up horizons to the infinite. Because its process of intensification is, in principle, unbounded, or so it would lead you to believe, hyperbole can only be understood relatively, in comparison to the ordinary discourse that it supersedes. However, it also denies the conventions which try to name it, the perspective of the ordinary from which it is recognized, analyzed, and explained. In a way, all good hyperboles resist explanation because they really mean what they say; a good hyperbole arrogantly sets a new standard of insight that rejects the logic of everyday discourse, refusing the very conditions from whence it arises. Hyperbole knows that it is not literally true, and yet it pursues its own logic of extremity in spite of this knowledge—for the sake of a different kind of truth.

Another aspect of this trope, the connection between figure and action, is not immediately evident and is the source of much confusion. Contrary to Marvick's insinuations, extravagant language does not necessarily lead to fanatical, or as the Enlightenment called it, "enthusiastic" behavior. The relationship between language and praxis in this case needs careful consideration. Some forms of hyperbolic discourse—say, the incitement to riot—do intend to create in reality what is said in language, yet other hyperboles are so obviously extreme and subtly sophisticated that they solicit reflection rather than invoke action, attract curiosity and suspicion, not enthusiasm. In this respect, it could be argued that good hyperboles contain within their own structure an ironic moment of hesitation and resistance. They both demand and warn, invite and refuse, insist and demur. The point is not only that praxis is not always such a clear reflection of language but also that excess can enlarge as well as restrict one's horizon for reflection and range of action. Religious hyperboles, I will argue, do not narrow but widen the imagination, multiplying and not limiting possibilities for action.

In this same context of the practical impact of this trope, an odd connection can be drawn between hyperbole and understatement, or litotes. Indeed, many hyperboles are deflated by leading to no action at all, or are translated into their opposite, the understatement.[28] Because excess is sometimes relatively easy to recognize, it can be quickly dismissed—the balloon, too full of air, pops—and nothing happens, nothing changes. Moderate arguments persuade; exaggerations shock, and after the shock—which results, after all, from a demand that cannot be met, a claim that is incredible—everything stays the same. By calling attention to its own extremity, hyperbole ironically makes the litotes look all the more reasonable. The hyperbole can thus function as a discharge of energy that does not direct action but rather makes action seem impossible and irrelevant. The result can be twofold. As a beguiling exuberance, hyperbole can serve not to guide action but to derail thought. Or by granting a glimpse of the impossible, hyperbole can make reality seem all the more necessary.

One way to think of hyperbole is with this image: it is the view from a peak which does not exist. This encapsulates both the grandeur but also the instability of the hyperbolic claim. Hyperbole surveys the horizon from an incredible perspective, but it is a perspective which does not have a solid basis in reality, ordinarily conceived. To extend this metaphor, one could say that the climb of exaggeration can be both exhausting and exhilarating, dangerous and sublime. It is an ascent that does not easily end because it leads to a point that is precariously steep and unfixed. One could also say that hyperbole is consent to a perspective from which certain views would not otherwise exist. By going too far, hyperbole is just right; its excess is just enough. Hyperbole is thus not mere exaggeration; it transgresses the logic of everyday language with some nonsense precisely when nothing else would make sense. Prima facie, this definition must seem paradoxical: Can hyperbole be both excessive and appropriate, too much and just enough, a wild, unruly, purposeless explosion and instructive, useful, even true? Does hyperbole conform to a rule? This question will inform all of my investigations, but it will especially surface in the chapter on G. K. Chesterton.

Perhaps the importance of hyperbole for many forms of discourse is questionable and doubtful, but I want to argue that for the religious spirit hyperbole is not an optional movement, a dispensable perspective. Religious claims often sound false today because religious persons do not speak them clearly; we hesitate, and qualify as we enunciate. The Enlightenment has taught religious persons to mumble, not exaggerate.[29] On the other hand, our society has assigned to hyperbole such a low standing that to speak religion directly, to hyperbolate religiously, is de facto to appear the fool. This is the dilemma of religion in the modern period: how to restore religion's proper voice when that voice has been muted, its integrity disfigured, its density diluted, to the point where it sounds, when it is heard at all, like a distant echo. How can a language be spoken that has been defined, in an a priori manner, as an embarrassment, an irrelevant and useless nuisance? Above all, today we need a new way to exclaim the unbelievable, to express the absurd, to make the impossible seem plausible, even necessary, and what better place to start than with the simple phrase, "God is love."

As Tracy's analysis suggests, the language of hyperbole is an appropriate articulation of the various genres of discourse in the New Testament. As his work also suggests, however, the word hyperbole itself, and the benefit of reflection on this trope, is rarely used to describe and explain New Testament discourse. Recently, many scholars have turned to rhetorical tropes, in particular metaphor, to understand biblical language more fully, but work on hyperbole has been sparse throughout the academy, and the field of biblical studies is no exception. Especially in religious studies, to talk about hyperbole can strike some people as a way of dismissing religious claims, reducing them to childish outpourings or unreflective clamor. To many people, hyperbole denotes falsity and crudity, so to mix hyperbole and religion is to deny any truth value—indeed, any respect—to the sober and somber claims of religion.

The analysis of exaggeration did serve a specific role in theology in recent history, but the approach used then impedes any attempt to employ the rhetoric of hyperbole today. In the nineteenth century, some liberal German biblical scholars began to interpret the miracle stories of the New Testament as exaggerations. When Jesus fed the thousands, they argued, perhaps he really fed only a few dozen, but the scene was so inspiring that later writers kept adding to the numbers until the miraculous element of Jesus' action became graphically clear. Albert Schweitzer's critical account of various quests for the historical Jesus is full of descriptions of such explanations of the miracle stories, even though the word exaggeration itself is rarely used. The great liberal historian Adolf von Harnack, however, makes explicit what others taught implicitly in his definition of the miraculous: "Stories which had their origin in an exaggerated view of natural events of an impressive character."[30] In other words, miracles are stories that have grown, through oral transmission, completely out of proportion to their original content; small surprises became, in the eyes of those who followed Jesus, great and mighty deeds.

Miracle stories are, therefore, mere exaggerations; they distort the facts and, moreover, are a stumbling block to the real, the literal, truth of Jesus' message. This interpretation does credit neither to hyperbole nor religion. It begins with a rationalistic assumption—the natural order is inviolable—and then proceeds to explain any transgression of that order as unwarranted but perhaps understandable. Ironically, exaggeration is used to show the inescapable dominance of the everyday, the ordinary and predictable. Exaggeration is thus given no positive meaning or significance of its own; it is merely a deviation, an aberration, and the only scholarly problem is to explain the origins of such abnormality. It is not a trope but a manner of deception, a product of intense wishes and a function of social needs but not an avenue into truth with its own integrity and dynamic.

Maybe it is natural to connect hyperbole to the miracle stories. After all, expressions of astonishment are recorded in the New Testament that could serve as the basis for a hyperbolic interpretation of these stories. After one miracle one gospel writer notes that the people went around saying, "We have seen strange things today" (Luke 5:26), spreading stories about Jesus. However, to call such stories exaggerations begs the question as to what exaggeration is. Moreover, who is to say where the exaggeration is located: in the telling of the story or in the power of Jesus? Finally, this whole discussion of the miraculous and exaggeration is limited by the desire to ascertain the literal truth or falsity of the miraculous event itself, a desire that not only cannot possibly be satisfied through linguistic analysis but also has nothing at all to do with exaggeration itself.

Of course, romantics like Friedrich Schleiermacher and Samuel Taylor Coleridge instinctively rejected the Enlightenment's displacement of excessive superstition with the claustrophobic and banal reign of unrestricted rationalism. They tried to resurrect the religious imagination by finding in nature and aesthetics the possibilities of mystery and transcendence. I want to confront the Enlightenment critique of exaggeration more directly. What is needed is a new perspective from which to view the relationship of religious event and exaggeration. A rehabilitation of hyperbole would direct enquiry not to ask about the reality that this figure distorts but rather the reality that could be expressed in no other way except through the excited and startling language of excess and extravagance. Hyperbole does not emphasize and magnify; it conjures and reveals.

An enlarged vision of hyperbole points in directions beyond the miracles debate. Jesus himself, after all, seemed to downplay his miracles in the New Testament; perhaps he knew how powerful such stories could become. His followers liked to tell miracle stories about him, but he himself liked to tell a different kind of story, what we call the parables. In moving away from the narrow confines of the miracles debate I want to try to substantiate my claim that hyperbole, once it is stripped of its negative connotations, does seem to pervade much religious discourse. In fact, hyperbole reaches its theological significance not in the miracle narratives but in Jesus' own words, in the parables.

Perhaps the pervasive use of hyperbole in the New Testament is so obvious that scholars are hesitant to pay attention to it. This, at any rate, is the theme of the one book on hyperbole and the Bible that I have been able to locate, a Ph.D. dissertation written by Claude Cicero Douglas in 1925, entitled *The Use of Hyperbole in the New Testament*.[31] I cite this work not as an example of how hyperbole should be used in biblical studies today—surely in such a fast-changing field its scholarly merit is virtually nil—nor as a prelude to further efforts in this regard, efforts for which I am neither qualified nor prepared. Nevertheless, this book is interesting to a theologian's reflections on rhetoric and religious language, and its conclusions about hyperbole do demand further reflection.

Douglas's theoretical discussion of hyperbole is not very helpful. He defines this trope as the figurative magnification of facts in the interest of a specific idea, thus reducing hyperbole to the meager gesture of emphasis. What is more interesting is his rejection of the vague umbrella label "figurative language" as a viable tool for biblical analysis; in its place he not only wants more specific rhetorical terms but also the particular trope of hyperbole. Nevertheless, after sharpening his focus to this one trope, he ends by finding it everywhere, a process of inflation that devalues his analysis: "So freely is this figure made use of in the New Testament that a mere citation of all the examples presents a bulk of material of such proportions as to surprise the Bible student who has not given special attention to this subject" (5). He pursues the "mere citation" ruthlessly and unrestrainedly, documenting literally hundreds of hyperboles throughout the New Testament, a procedure that forces one to wonder why these examples have not been properly labeled before. Students of the Bible miss these exaggerations, he surmises, because we are too familiar with these sayings and because "we unconsciously reduced the proportions of the objects represented to meet the requirements of reason" (6).

By connecting hyperbole to the miracle stories Douglas betrays his firm entrenchment in nineteenth-century liberal theology. With the advantage of hindsight, he suggests, modern people can distinguish between literal and exaggerated fact, an inability that allowed the biblical writers to express their conviction of God's presence in exaggerations of physical phenomena. Fortunately, Douglas does move on to hyperbolic analyses of other biblical texts, especially the sayings of Jesus. In fact, "In the use of hyperbole Jesus surpassed all others whose teachings are recorded in the New Testament" (66). After raising the question of who was responsible for the exaggerations of these sayings, Jesus or his followers, Douglas speculates that many of Jesus' statements were remembered and recorded because of their exaggerated features. In fact, he hypothesizes that the more hyperbolic the New Testament statement, the more likely it is genuinely attributable to Jesus.

The scholarly questions raised here are complex and profound, beyond the reach of both Douglas and me. This book does, however, open up a line of reflection that is not that far removed from the conclusions of Tracy's article about religious language, and its focus on hyperbole is bold and original, both for its time and our own. There is an excess to many of Jesus' teachings and stories that is both troubling and enduring. Jesus told stories which were so fantastic that he cautioned his followers to come to him as children, wide-eyed, as it were. How many times should you forgive somebody? Can a rich man enter the kingdom of God? Who is our neighbor? Does God really love us? To all of these questions Jesus told stories that could only strike their hearers as extravagant, using what G. K. Chesterton has aptly described as a "gigantesque diction."[32]

The central message of these parables, as Tracy and many commentators have pointed out, seems to be the simple assertion of the boundless love of God. That love is so unfathomable and so wonderful that Jesus frequently turns to striking, excessive, and bold images to portray it. To paraphrase these parables would not do them justice; to analyze a selection of them is outside the scope of this chapter. Instead, I want to focus on the seemingly simple claim that God is love, a powerfully direct condensation of the insight of many of the parables. A central question immediately arises: Is this statement a religious fact that the parables expand and embellish, or is it too rhetorically constructed? According to Tracy, it is a root metaphor, a fusion of elements that, though metaphorical itself, serves to structure and generate other, more detailed metaphors and narratives. What would it mean to interpret this statement as hyperbole?

Interestingly, one theologian has recently recognized this formulation of Christian piety, that God is love, as precisely an exaggeration. James Gustafson has written,

Both Christian piety and Christian theology have had excessive confidence in the divine goodness toward individuals and communities, and toward our species...But I reject the notion of trust as ultimate confidence that God intends my individual good as the usually inflated and exaggerated terms portray that good.[33]

Gustafson is afraid that Christians often reduce the claim that God is love to the exaggeration of the ultimate worth and value of the individual regardless of the value of others (whether other humans or other species). He wants a more sober, a more realistic assessment of God's love and human value. He wants a religious language that will do justice to the precarious place of humanity in the cosmos and the complex range of feelings, chiefly dependence, creatures have for their creator.

Much of his work is dedicated to analyzing the evidence for the character of God from our experiences of nature and other selves. Our knowledge of God, he argues, must be strictly correlated to what we actually know and feel, what he calls our piety. Gustafson's method is intriguing and challenging; the God he infers from experience, a God who does not place human salvation at the center of the divine drama, is often at odds with Christian orthodoxy. All of nature is involved in Gustafson's conception of God's mercy; God is at the center, not humanity, and humanity does not receive any special privileges from God. Gustafson raises many fascinating issues, and his ecological concerns are commendable, but for my purposes, he underlines the excess of the claim that God is love by showing it to be without foundation in human experience. In a revealing comment, he notes, "One could make love the exclusive predicate of God only by vastly ballooning its meaning."[34] I want to say: precisely.

More traditional Christian theologians have not wanted to qualify and moderate the bold statement that

God is love.[35] In fact, Gustafson's position makes traditional religious language seem to be what it is, that is, extravagant; as John H. Yoder has commented, "To say of God so defined [by Gustafson] that 'He' can be 'glorified' or 'obeyed' has become an excessive and substantively empty metaphor."[36] Indeed, the very problem that plagues Gustafson, the nature of human experience, has led many theologians to the opposite of his conclusion, to emphasize the love of God all the more, not less. One of the best ways to understand the extravagance of the claim that God is love is through an analysis of the problem of evil, the most difficult of human experiences. Philosophers often debate the problem of evil as if evil is incompatible with a good and omnipotent God. The question thus becomes one of theodicy, or the justification of God: Why does God allow evil, especially unwarranted human suffering, to occur? To be blunt, if God is love, and all-powerful love at that, why evil?

To understand "God is love" as hyperbole is to see it not as a fact that contradicts the experience of evil but as an extravagance that makes evil existentially livable, if not theoretically resolvable. Evil is the fact, the experience that makes the hyperbole of God's love all the more clearly excessive. Evil makes God's love both necessary and impossible. Gustafson is correct that we do not directly and unequivocally experience God as loving; such a belief breaks out of the ordinary boundaries of our experience. To ground this belief in the evidence of human suffering would be foolish, an insult to the victims of evil. To ground this belief in the experience of human limitations would be equally inappropriate, an attempt to squeeze a surplus into a container too small to hold it. To say God is love is to speak of an experience that is a remainder when all such evil has been thoroughly documented and condemned, when all limitations have been recognized and registered. To use the paradoxical language of deconstructionism, God's love is a trace that can be followed only due to its very absence.

Evil itself, it is important to note, has a strong connection to hyperbole. Primo Levi has told the story of how the survivors of the Holocaust at first often did not speak because they thought they would not be believed. Indeed, survivors and historians alike were frequently accused of exaggerations. The public was inclined to reject the brutal fact of the Holocaust because of its very enormity. As Levi explains, "Even if we were to tell it, we would not be believed."[37] We nonsurvivors refuse to believe the unbelievable even when it is all too true. We do not want human evil to break the boundaries of the credible, the expected, the known. All evil, no matter how very real it is, strikes us as an excess that defies the laws of reason and civility.

Because we try to minimize the reality of evil, just as we minimize the love of God, talk about evil often strikes us as exaggerated, as a discourse that is uncomfortably related to the other languages we easily speak. The exaggeration of God's love and evil are not identical, one is more obviously evident than the other, and yet both realities require articulations that are frequently unbelievable in their extravagance. Love and evil are extremes that lie at opposite ends of the spectrum of human existence. The hope of love is that, perhaps somewhere, extremes meet, that love does conquer, judge, and redeem evil and its consequences. Such love is neither a rationalization nor a calculation but is like a dimly glimpsed dream felt through a sorrowful awakening, a memory that precedes belief.

For many, this dream has receded to an unarticulated background, repressed and forgotten. Our skeptical and ironic culture teaches us to squint at everything, to combat the fear of being naive, of being deceived: we want to believe less, not more. Indeed, today sobriety jealously governs the languages that most of us speak. We North Americans are a pragmatic people, suspicious of extremes, careful and cautious in politics and religion alike. Marvick is wrong to worry about a hyperbole freed from ironic restraint; our situation is just the opposite. In fact, the forces of the world work to reverse the dangerous effect of religious excess, as Pascal noted long ago: "Imagination magnifies small objects with fantastic exaggeration until they fill our soul, and with bold insolence cuts down great things to its own size, as when speaking of God."[38] North American pragmatism too often makes of God an understatement, while the anxiety of survival magnifies all of the details of day-to-day existence to such a degree that we can see nothing else. Enthusiasm today is limited to very specific fields of public activity, like sports or, to some extent, specific political issues, but otherwise, enthusiasm should be kept private, especially the enthusiasm of religion.

Nevertheless, there seems to be something wonderfully extravagant about religion that can serve to disrupt the everyday caution of ordinary discourse. Indeed, for some people the fact of evil without God's love would be unbearable. The blessed excess of God's love lures people into an extravagant mode that defies the facts of existence. To be specific, the Christian response to God's love must be a willingness to see God as more present in the world than our ordinary experience would lead us to believe. The wide eyes of Christian love do not see everything; those eyes see only God's love, and thus are willing to trust and to forgive, to hope and to care, even in the midst of rejection and despair. Even if nothing good can be found in a situation, even if all appearances point to the opposite of love, love still loves, without fear of being deceived. Love believes all (good) things, hopes all things, forgives all things. (See 1 Corinthians 13:7). It is the string of "alls" in that statement that makes love both wonderful and terrifying.[39]

How this simple assertion works what Nietzsche called "the magic of the extreme"[40] is not easy to say. True, exaggerations often come in clusters of bombastic and even garish prose, spread out through an accumulation of inordinate claims and proliferated through striking images. In contrast, the structure of the phrase "God is love" is apparently simple, but such simplicity is deceiving; indeed, the little "is" hides a depth of meaning. That little "is"—God *is* love—promotes love to the highest imaginable rank. It is an imperious copula, which stubbornly resists all hesitations and retractions with the finality of an almost mathematical equation. To identify God with love is not to create an artful metaphorical image where before only a vague sensation prevailed, an image that makes no exclusive claims to truth. Instead, the hyperbolic "is" denies the metaphorical "as if" and the analogical "like" with a bluntness that says not that God is loving but that God is love itself, that love is the proper name of God.

In this identification the value of both terms are radically altered. Indeed, the hyperbole leads along a direction of thought that we want to qualify and modify. We think we know what love is, but then it is elevated to identify God. We have many ideas about God, but then those ideas are focused, concentrated, and distilled into the one word of love. We want to say that God is many other things besides love; we want to say that love is not worthy of this honor, to reside with God. We want to say that, at best, God is like love, so to speak. The hyperbole, however, provides not an image but the demand that we verify this exacting identification in our own personal experience. To say "God is love," then, commits us to an extravagant willingness to find God wherever we discover love, and to see in the practice of love the work of God—and to find both God and love more present than appearances would ever allow.

At the risk of being prosaic, I want to suggest four implications of a hyperbolic imagination of the extremes of God's loving grace.[41] First, we are impelled to seek love everywhere, because God is everywhere. Such a search is never ending, but it can be bold and open nonetheless, stretching our horizons even beyond our imaginations to find ever new possibilities for love. Second, where we find love, we can know we have found

God. We are ennobled to celebrate and affirm those possibilities that extend beyond our best efforts and come
to us like unexpected and surprising gifts. Third, when
we love, we know that our love will be everlasting. The
identification of God and love points to the abiding persistence of love itself, over and above the transitory
nature of our own finite and fallible attempts to love.
Fourth, when we fail to find love, and fail to love, we
know that nevertheless love persists, and so we can forgive as we already have been forgiven, love because we
are loved already. We can find the courage to love that
transcends the calculative mind-set of the modern
world. In sum, notice the difference between the disorienting but enlarging power of "God is love" and the more
mundane and common, "God loves you"; the former
transforms our understanding of love by stretching it
toward God, while the latter risks reducing God to a
means of strengthening the already egocentric self.

   This paraphrase of the hyperbole of love is meant to
be suggestive, not exhaustive. If "God is love" is a good
hyperbole, it will serve to expand visions and upset
prejudices, activities not easily definable. Indeed, I
hope that my discussion has corrected the impression
that hyperboles are facile and transparent, as opposed
to the finesse and subtlety of good metaphors. Marvick
blames the low standing of hyperbole among the tropes,
its illegitimacy, on its directness: "If twentieth century
critics have not appreciated the full meaning of hyperbole, it is doubtless because they have clung too tena-
ciously to their ability to see through it" (60). Hyperbole
is thus too easy; in other words, it does not give rise to a
sufficient amount of interpretive complexity, the kind
of thing upon which academic criticism rests.[42]

   Metaphors do seem to be more delicate than hyperboles; they can be considered a horizontal trope, carefully drawing together two disparate realms, while the
verticality of hyperbole extends one realm as far as it
will go. Hyperbole can thus seem more mannered,[43]
more intentional and less nuanced than metaphor. The

single-mindedness of the hyperbole does not want to make a new identification (the metaphorical "as if") but to see how far an observation can be taken when stripped of all reservation and qualification. It seeks not to synthesize but to stretch, not to persuade but to shock. Instead of extending, it jolts the imagination. At times, however, it is precisely this kind of abrupt escalation that is needed to alter a perspective, challenge an assumption, or extend the imagination a bit further than it would otherwise want to go. Such excesses will frequently appear groundless, rushing headstrong on to nowhere, confusing reality with what could or should but seemingly cannot be. The more we resist, though, the stronger good hyperboles pull, and we *can* follow, conscious of our fear of being thought foolish, of believing too much, of going too far.

Chapter Two

More Than Too Much:
Kierkegaard's *Works of Love* Revisited

It is a strange thing to note the excess of this passion, and how it braves the nature and value of things, by this; that the speaking in a perpetual hyperbole is comely in nothing but love.
—Francis Bacon, "Of Love,"
Essays or Counsels Civil and Moral

We pay a heavy, very heavy price for the superhuman dignity of our calling. The ridiculous is always so near to the sublime. And the world, usually so indulgent to foibles, hates ours instinctively.
—Georges Bernanos,
The Diary of a Country Priest

Søren Kierkegaard's *Works of Love* is one of his most moving and accessible books. In it he asserts the power and purity of Christian love: it obliterates all distinctions, takes the form of self-sacrifice, and is best actualized in the nonrefundable love for the dead. "The great exponent of extremity"[1] is uncompromising in his portrayal of the unlimited demands of Christlike love. His tenacity has raised many questions in the secondary literature: Can the Christian really love *everyone*, without qualification or distinction? Does Kierkegaard go too far? I want to argue that these commonsense demurrals

33

misread Kierkegaard's position. Recent studies have increasingly emphasized the rhetorical features of Kierkegaard's writings. I want to claim that his work on love—what has been called a total morality[2]—should be best understood from the perspective of hyperbole. Kierkegaard not only makes exaggerated claims about the nature and purpose of Christian love but also portrays such love as hyperbole itself: love always goes too far and gives too much. If discourse about love is to meet the demands of Christianity, then it cannot say too much, cannot be too extravagant—cannot be anything but hyperbole.

The most careful critique of Kierkegaard's excessive position, a response which typifies much of the secondary literature, can be found in Gene Outka's *Agape, An Ethical Analysis*.[3] Outka argues that Kierkegaard reduces the varieties of love to the one dimension of agape, or equal regard for all others. This exclusive concern for agape, Outka claims, does not do justice to preferential relationships like friendship or erotic love. Indeed, the high vantage point of agape regards any mutuality or reciprocity in a loving relationship with suspicion. Only sacrifice can deliver a love free of all traces of self-interest. Such self-renunciation cannot, by its own logic, prefer to serve one person or group of people over another. True love, then, in Outka's reading of Kierkegaard, must be indiscriminate.

Outka articulates an impressive range of objections both to Kierkegaard's position and to theologians influenced by him, like Reinhold Niebuhr and Anders Nygren. A listing of some of these objections should be sufficient to show the prima facie unreasonableness of Kierkegaard's approach. Should one be willing to help everyone indiscriminately, Outka asks? He calls this the problem of the blank check. "For love is absent when one party does all the giving and the other all the taking" (36). Moreover, personal relationships are limited, he argues, by considerations of mutuality. This restriction, the mutual willingness to enter into the relationship, is crucial: one cannot help people against their will. Considerations of mutuality lead to the conclusion that every single relationship has special demands and needs that cannot be extrapolated to include other relationships.

Finally, Outka suggests that Kierkegaard disregards the possibility of a proper self-love as well as a harmonious sharing with others. Kierkegaard's focus on self-sacrifice presupposes a society in conflict in which personal relationships are tensely based on competing interests. If interests coincide, Outka seems to be suggesting, then self-love and mutuality might supplant or at least supplement self-sacrifice. This argument is especially forceful due to recent feminist analyses of sacrifice as a particularly masculine virtue, a counterbalance to the aggressive male ego; women, on the other hand, have practiced sacrifice often to their own detriment, and now need to find ways of self-assertion and affirmation instead.[4] The rhetoric of sacrifice thus masks a rhetoric of domination and oppression.

The impact of Outka's analysis is that Kierkegaard, by rejecting any consideration of the other's response to love, comes dangerously close to treating the neighbor as "little more than an *occasion* for disclosing the state of the agent" (280). That conclusion is echoed in another important critique of Kierkegaard's excesses. Theodor W. Adorno, in an essay devoted exclusively to *Works of Love*, indicts Kierkegaard for an extreme subjectivism that finally makes no room for love of the other.[5] Adorno recognizes the special place that this book occupies in the Kierkegaardian corpus: it supplements his negative theology with a positive position, his criticisms with edification, and his dialectics with simple expressions. Nevertheless, Adorno thinks that the book is too long, repetitive, verbose, and loquacious. He sees this as part of Kierkegaard's rhetorical strategy: "If the philosophical writings wish to 'cheat' the reader into the truth, the theological ones, in turn, wish to make it as difficult, as uninteresting, as insipid

to him as possible" (21). This perceptive comment on
the style of *Works of Love* points to its hyperbolic form:
it is not an ironic work which deceives the reader;
rather, it presents love in such a strenuous way that the
actualization of love seems impossible. In fact, Adorno
claims that, "Kierkegaard never concretely states what
this love means" (21), but uses negative analogies to
show how this love is always something different from
what we might expect or want.

Like Outka, Adorno is most concerned that Kierkegaard does not make distinctions in the questions of
who and how to love. "Speaking exaggeratedly," he
writes, "in Kierkegaard's doctrine of love the object of
love is, in a way, irrelevant" (21). The exaggeration is
Kierkegaard's, not Adorno's. Kierkegaard, Adorno claims,
develops an objectless love whose rigor matches, if it
does not surpass, Kant's notorious sense of duty. Love
breaks down nature; one's inclinations should not affect
it. Happiness is love's worst disfigurement. The result,
Adorno claims, is a devaluation of the loved person. The
lover comes close to a callous kind of recklessness, a
spiritualization of love which overstrains itself and
threatens to turn into its opposite, hate. In the end,
"Kierkegaard's doctrine remains totally abstract" (24).
Adorno thinks that by going too far such love does not
go far enough.

The neighbor is Kierkegaard's concrete category for
the person to be loved, but for Adorno Kierkegaard's discourse remains too general. He accuses Kierkegaard of
reducing the neighbor to the general principle of otherness or to the universally human: "The particular reality
which I encounter in my neighbor is thus rendered
totally accidental" (25). The only criterion for love is the
pure inwardness of the lover, not the needs of the loved
one. This is, Adorno argues, an impotent mercifulness
which is far removed from the Gospels' privileging of the
poor, the fishermen and the publicans. Worst of all,
Adorno claims, Kierkegaard repeats the Lutheran doctrine of compartmentalizing the two kingdoms of God

and humanity and thus advocating total obedience to the state. There is no social substance to Kierkegaard's interiorized love which, indeed, assumes the maintenance of the status quo. What is needed, Adorno laments, is a breaking of the capitalist reduction of love to exchange, a process which he analyzes in detail in his later work with Max Horkheimer, *Dialectic of the Enlightenment.*[6]

Adorno's Marxist perspective seems to have collided with Kierkegaard's Christianity, and yet, in the middle of this article there is a surprising, and late, statement of Adorno's thesis: "Kierkegaard's misanthropy, the paradoxical callousness of his doctrine of love enables him, like few other writers, to perceive decisive character features of the typical individual of modern society" (28). Kierkegaard, in spite of himself, seems to have stumbled upon the truth of the contemporary situation. Adorno is driven to this admission by Kierkegaard's own insightful analysis of the decay of Christianity in Western culture, a decay that shows the progress of the West to result only in the reification of personal relationships and the domination of suffocating social conventions. For Adorno, Kierkegaard's impotency reflects the social fact that the neighbor no longer exists, that there is nothing we can do for any concrete other. The Christian command of love has become totally incompatible with present social structures. The excess of Kierkegaard's position—his utopian tendencies—are a protest against the impossibility of true individualism in a mass culture. In capitalism, life is reduced to reproduction and human relations reflect the dynamic of the process of exchange, or bartering. Kierkegaard's celebration of love for the dead, then, is ironically an authentic but desperate caricature of the only unmutilated love possible in our society: "The paradox that the only true love is love for the dead is the perfect expression of our situation" (32). Kierkegaard has gone too far because there was nowhere else he could go.

It is not my intention to answer these charges on

Kierkegaard's behalf in any detail. Indeed, the reasonableness of many of these disclaimers seems to me to
be self-evident. The critiques of both writers converge
on Kierkegaard's excesses, Outka asking for qualifications and Adorno suggesting that, at best, these
excesses are utopian in an age when no other action is
possible and, at worst, they represent an impotent
revolt which reflects the failure of society as a whole.
Both writers accuse Kierkegaard of abstraction by talking about the neighbor in terms that are too general and
not grounded in, for Outka, issues of mutuality or, for
Adorno, critical accounts of social structures. To be fair,
I should note that both writers recognize that there is
liberating potential in Kierkegaard's position. For
Adorno, however, it is a liberation that is constrained
by a society that does not allow for better alternatives,
and thus it is an illusion; for Outka, the demanding
character of Kierkegaard's love is praiseworthy, but it
can be better expressed in more modest terms.

     In this chapter I want to make the case that such cor-
rective comments are beside the point in the same way
that any attempt to read a hyperbolic discourse literally
can be accused of misreading. Indeed, these misread-
ings try to resist the excesses of Kierkegaard's work and
thus point the way to a proper reading. *That which is
resisted is hyperbole.* This claim is actually situated in
the mainstream of much of the recent literature on
Kierkegaard, studies that have focused on his rhetoric,
especially the irony of his frequently untrustworthy
pseudonyms and the humor of his excessively dialectical deliberations.[7] Kierkegaard himself frequently wrote
about irony, and, to a lesser extent, he also wrote about
hyperbole. While Kierkegaard's irony has received extensive treatment, his hyperbole has rarely been analyzed,
even though it is difficult to read his attack upon Christendom or his insistence on the absolute paradox of
faith as anything but species of that trope.

     This should not be surprising. Hyperbole is a
neglected trope. Its logic is difficult to define because it

breaks through the ordinary decorum of language, and it is frequently irritating or ridiculous in the extremity of its claims. Yet hyperbole can speak truth. Adorno, himself a great hyperbolist, acknowledged the connection between hyperbole and his own negative dialectics: "It [thought] expresses exactly what is, precisely because what is is never quite as thought expresses it. Essential to it is an element of exaggeration, of overshooting the object, of self-detachment from the weight of the factual, so that instead of merely reproducing being it can, at once rigorous and free, determine it."[8] This definition of hyperbole, the saying too much in order to say just enough when everything else is insufficient, will guide my own reading of Kierkegaard's *Works of Love*.

Kierkegaard's writings are so complex and deceptive that no single passage illuminates the whole. Yet a comment in the book *Repetition* can serve as an entry into his exaggerated prose. The narrator, Constantine Constantius, himself an admittedly untrustworthy character, is speaking about "A," the author of *Either/Or*: "Recollection's love is the only happy love, says an author who, as far as I know him, is at times somewhat deceitful, not in the sense that he says one thing and means another [read: irony] but in the sense that he pushes the thought to extremes, so that if it is not grasped with the same energy, it reveals itself the next instant as something else."[9] This confession—which, I will soon argue, applies to more of Kierkegaard's work than just the pseudonymous "A"—reflects another of Adorno's comments on hyperbole: "The dialectic [Adorno's own as opposed to Hegel's] advances by way of extremes, driving thoughts with the utmost consequentiality to the point where they turn back on themselves, instead of qualifying them."[10] Both authors agree that in certain situations only extremity can speak truth even though they use that extremity in different ways. For Adorno, hyperbole manifests itself as the refusal ever to accept any single argument as final, or conversely, the desire to disconnect critique from any

conception of the whole, from any positive or constructive telos. For Kierkegaard, hyperbole takes the form of
extreme claims which also derail thinking but eventuate
in a demand for action, not further and never ending
reflection.

Both Adorno and Kierkegaard are driven to hyperbole by their refusal to accept the status quo. Their
rhetorics cannot begin with the needs and desires of
their audiences. For Kierkegaard, the triumphs of Christianity, and the allegedly vast numbers of Christians,
have been so exaggerated that becoming a Christian, in a
so-called Christian culture, is no longer a task but rather
an assumption. In *The Present Age* he argues—and
laments—that people have lost their passion and therefore merely believe what everyone else believes. Society
has been leveled flat by resentment and envy, and the
abstract category of the public has replaced concrete
individuality. People exaggerate the greatness of Christianity only because they then may be excused from following that which is so soberly elevated. Excessive
praise is perfectly correlated with an unwillingness to
act. Kierkegaard wants to fight these disabling exaggerations with a harsher and yet ultimately more enabling
discourse.

Kierkegaard's own self-awareness of his stylistic
strategy is not difficult to decipher. For example, in the
midst of *Training in Christianity*, where he portrays discipleship with Jesus Christ as a marvelous madness, an
incredible impossibility which is still yet a demand, he
says (or almost murmurs) in an aside: "Oh, say not that
this whole treatment is an exaggeration."[11] And in *The
Sickness unto Death* he admits that his talk about
despair will strike many as overstatement.[12] In this
book he claims that such excess cannot be avoided
when one talks about the offense of Christianity which
breaks with human wisdom.

Too little and too much spoil everything. This is
bandied about among men as wisdom, is honored

with admiration; its exchange rate never fluctuates, and all mankind guarantees its worth. Now and then there is a genius who goes a little way beyond this, and he is called crazy—by sensible people. But Christianity makes an enormous giant stride beyond this *ne quid nimis* [nothing too much] into the absurd; that is where Christianity begins—and offense. (86-7)

Nothing too much: the classical wisdom of moderation, the virtue of the Greeks, is at the root of the end of Christianity and the beginning of Christendom. Ironically, by claiming that Christianity has triumphed and that everybody is a Christian, crude exaggerations at best, Christianity has been attenuated of any positive meaning whatsoever—precisely by those who call themselves Christians. Now the true Christian is forced to go too far, to say too much, to be, in an un-Greek manner, absurd, in order to say anything or do anything at all. This coincidence of the "too far" and the "just right" in Kierkegaard's use of hyperbole demonstrates the irreducible integrity and cognitive validity of this trope.

Kierkegaard's response to these exaggerations of Christianity's successes is to exaggerate just the opposite. This corrective exaggeration will not lead to the virtue of moderation but rather the scandal of the absurd. Note that Kierkegaard does not reduce Christian belief to exaggeration itself, as he makes clear in that wonderfully single-minded text, *Purity of Heart*: "Now willing one thing does not mean to commit the grave mistake of a brazen, unholy enthusiasm, namely, to will the big, no matter it be good or bad."[13] True Christianity must be the proper exaggeration of believing not what everybody else believes, that is, the impressive and the popular, but believing that which cannot be believed, the impossible, the offense.

The controversial *The Point of View for My Work as an Author*, a text whose credibility has been frequently challenged, contains Kierkegaard's most complete dis-

cussion of hyperbole.[14] Written in 1848 but not published until 1859, this work portrays Kierkegaard's
authorship as one long inevitable as well as circuitous
unfolding of the religious point of view, a reading
which some scholars think is a rationalization rather
than a description of a program planned from the very
beginning. What I find most interesting about this book
is its reflections on rhetoric. Kierkegaard interprets his
past literary production in terms not only of religion
but also of irony. He has attacked Christendom, he
claims, only indirectly, not saying what he has really
meant. Indeed, direct action, which he discusses under
the rubric of hyperbole, would not have worked: "Once
in a while there appears a religious enthusiast: he
storms against Christendom, he vociferates and makes
a loud noise, denouncing almost all as not being Christians—and accomplishes nothing" (24). Hyperbole is a
desperate strategy, used only when all other means of
communication have failed.

Such enthusiasm will not stir Christians from their
slumber; in fact, the hyperbolist will be called "a
fanatic, his Christianity an exaggeration—in the end he
remains the only one, or one of the few, who is not seriously a Christian (for exaggeration is surely a lack of
seriousness), whereas the others are all serious Christians" (24). Christendom makes direct discourse about
Christianity impossible, or rather, direct discourse will
itself appear to be hyperbolic. Ironically, the result is
that the exaggerator will not be taken seriously, even
though he or she has been forced into exaggeration by
the pervasive mediocrity and complacency of Christendom. To dispel the illusion of Christendom, an indirect
attack is needed: "A direct attack only strengthens a
person in his illusion, and at the same time embitters
him" (25). Extremity begets extremity; only deception
can cure the deceived.

Ironically, after Kierkegaard wrote this book he
turned increasingly to hyperbole, to a pointed attack,
and away from his pseudonymous deceptions. His blast

against the church, which took place at the end of his life, in 1854 and 1855, was nothing but exaggeration, as Walter Lowrie realized in a bit of understatement: "One-sidedness, he thought, and even a dose of exaggeration was necessary for the effect he desired to produce."[15] This explosion against the church was itself an extravagant deception, and many people took this attack, especially when it turned personally against the highly respected Bishop Mynster and professor and later Bishop Martensen, literally. After all, hyperbole, especially in polemical contexts, is the most direct of the figures, a characteristic that can confuse both its launching and its reception. Indeed, it is a remark on the low standing of hyperbole among the tropes that even those scholars who recognize that Kierkegaard's attack was in the form of hyperbole still think it is a direct, in the sense of nonfigural, discourse and thus debate its relationship to his earlier, indirect (ironic) discourse. His contemporaries were also confused by his diatribes: Was he attacking the church from within or without? Kierkegaard knew that the purest impact of hyperbole could only be achieved if his broadsides were left unqualified, unexplained. He wanted to disorient his readers, to leave them without their usual props of ready-made answers and easy rationalizations. Hyperbole was Kierkegaard's last pseudonym, and like every good trope it had to stand on its own.

Works of Love, written in 1847, anticipates this shift from irony to hyperbole.[16] Here Kierkegaard is concerned not to draw his readers into Christianity gradually, through deception, but rather to confront them with a Christianity that shatters and explodes all of their beliefs and practices. This work is not hyperbolic in exactly the same way as the final paroxysm against Christendom, but it does help prepare for that attack by showing Christianity to be in drastic discontinuity with what the world already believes. Christian love, Kierkegaard argues, is not a higher form of a diluted but still respectable natural, secular love. Agape is not worn out eroticism. This fact is crucial to Kierkegaard's rhetorical strategy, as he makes clear in his *Journal*:

> An edifying discourse about love presupposes that men know essentially what love is and seeks to win them to it, to move them. But this is in fact not the case. Therefore the 'reflections' must first fetch them up out of the cellar, call to them, turn their comfortable way of thinking topsy-turvy with the dialectic of truth.[17]

The dialectic of truth advances on several fronts, attacking in seemingly confused directions, without any obvious plan or goal. In a *Journal* entry about *Works of Love* Kierkegaard defines his anti-Hegelian dialectic in terms that anticipate Adorno's exaggerated negations: "When I have first presented one aspect sharply and clearly, then I affirm the validity of the other even more strongly."[18] Kierkegaard's dialectic does not take both sides of a position for the purposes of circumspection and moderation. Indeed, talk about love risks running out of control because it cannot describe what is; instead, it must speak about what is not, about the impossible, and yet it must speak about it in such a way that it is a possibility, a possibility that always entices but eludes our reach.

A dialectic that pushes beyond itself only to retreat (or attack?) in the opposite direction will necessarily be a long and sometimes tedious process. Indeed, the length of *Works of Love* is itself part of the intended exaggeration, as Adorno suggests, an attempt to force self-examination by impeding any quick reception. As the translators note in their introduction, "The development of the reflections moves towards closing escape hatches and running down equivocations and uncovering evasions as it sharpens distinctions and lays bare explications in concepts and existential positions" (14). The laborious length of the work reflects the endless and relentless task of love itself.

A crucial comment in Kierkegaard's foreword makes all of this somewhat more clear: "That which in its vast abundance is essentially inexhaustible is also essentially indescribable in its smallest act, simply because essentially it is everywhere wholly present and essentially cannot be described" (19). Love is both obvious and otherworldly. The repetition of "essentially" here is not meant to mark a discourse which strives for definition, nor is it meant to caution discourse from trying to pry into unknown secrets or hidden essences. Instead, Kierkegaard is saying that his own discourse can never say enough about that which can never be exhausted; he must, therefore, write with an abandon about this abundance. He is forced to exaggerate.

It is appropriate that this work begins with a reflection on deception. Kierkegaard recognizes that most people have an inordinate fear of being deceived. People do not want to be caught believing something that is not true; cleverness thus guards against naïveté. To the predominance of this line of thinking Kierkegaard raises the following objection: If we believe only what we can see, that about which we are certain, then we could never believe in love. Indeed, such skepticism would itself be the greatest deception. It is true that love cuts across common sense; Kierkegaard never tires of repeating that one can do quite well in the world without Christian love. Christian love, however, is not for the clever. In fact, love is defined precisely in terms of hyperbole as that force which wills to believe always more and never less: "If mistrust can see something as less than it actually is, love can see something as greater than it is" (33). Love always sees more and believes more than what is 'really' there, yet it is an easy victim to skepticism because there is no rational basis for its excesses.

Nor is love for those who, out of a fear of being hypocrites, act moderately without excessive claims or visions. "The most mediocre defence against hypocrisy is prudence; well, it is hardly a defence, rather a dan-

gerous neighbor of hypocrisy. The best defence against
hypocrisy is love; yes, it is not only a defence but a
yawning abyss; in all eternity it has nothing to do with
hypocrisy" (32). The jumbled leaps in this comment follow the leaps which love itself demands. Prudence is a
defense against love which succeeds only too well. Love
itself is not a defence against anything but rather an
abyss—an abyss which threatens to swallow all of our
rationalizations and hesitations.

A modest, cautious discourse would merely whis-
per into this abyss. With love, another tone of voice is
demanded: "Concerning relationships of the spirit, one
cannot—if one wants to avoid talking foolishly—talk
like a shopkeeper who has the best grade of goods and
in addition a medium grade, which he can also highly
recommend as being almost as good" (59). This is the
nature of a superlative discourse: all comparisons
break down as love is elevated to a status uniquely its
own. "Christianity does not lead you up to some better
place, from which you nevertheless can only survey a
somewhat wider territory—this is still only an earthly
hope and a worldly vision" (233). No matter how highly
you praise love, no matter how wonderful you think
love is, agape always goes further than that. This is an
insight into the nature of hyperbole itself: it does not
praise by degrees but by leaps and bounds; it does not
talk about the highest, but about that which is higher
than all talk about height itself.

A good example of how Kierkegaard's hyperbole
shapes his text is his interpretation of the biblical
demand, "You shall love your neighbor as yourself." For
Kierkegaard, the key question is, What does the "as
yourself" mean? Here he rejects Outka's interpretation
that this passage implies the possibility of a proper self
love. Instead, he reads the "as" as "instead." In other
words, as you would want to love yourself, instead love
your neighbor. There is, then, no room here for a love
of self. "But this *as yourself*—yes, no wrestler can wrap
himself around his opponent as this command wraps

itself about self-love, which cannot move from the spot"
(35). As, I might add, Kierkegaard's book tries to wrap
itself around the reader, not leaving self-love "the
slightest excuse or the tiniest escape-hatch" (34–5).

   In a similar fashion Kierkegaard rereads the parables about the Good Samaritan and the poor woman
who gave a few pennies to the temple treasury. In a
poetic variation he imagines that the innkeeper did not
accept the sick man whom the Samaritan found, or the
sick man died in the Samaritan's arms. He also wonders
what the reader would think if the poor woman had had
her pennies stolen and gave away an empty purse, even
though she did not realize its emptiness. These parables, of course, already portray the importance of loving and giving regardless of the consequences. Kierkegaard's intensifications make this point even more
strongly. Like Kant, he thinks that love is only true if it
suffers, without reward, deprived of happiness. He concludes his poetic experiment with the brutally unqualified comment: "Mercifulness is able to do nothing"
(299). With that statement he wholeheartedly affirms
the impotence which to Adorno is his most crippling
vulnerability.

   Perhaps Kierkegaard's hyperbolic understanding of
love is most clearly formulated in his reflection on the
Corinthian passage that love believes, hopes, and
endures all things (1 Corinthians 13:7). Here Kierkegaard returns to his favorite topic of deception. "To
believe all things means precisely, even though love is
not apparent, even though the opposite is seen, to presuppose that love is nevertheless present fundamentally, even in the misguided, even in the corrupt, even in
the hateful" (209). This love can believe abundantly
without fear of being deceived because it presupposes
the triumph of love. It is not believing because of "frivolity, inexperience, simplicity, which believe all things on
the grounds of naivete and ignorance" (216). The true
lover cannot be deceived "for to deceive him is to
deceive oneself" (225) out of love. Love has no founda-

tions; it is not dependent on anything else. It presupposes itself. Evil, therefore, cannot alter it. Love sees
evil, but it does not deign to acknowledge its reality.
Indeed, the hyperbole of love combats evil, because, "To
believe nothing is right on the border where believing
evil begins..." (220). In fact, through forgiveness love
defeats evil by hiding, in a cunning act of resistance, the
multiplicity of sins. In this way love abides, an
endurance caught by this sharp image: "Imagine a com-
pound word which lacks the last word; there is only the
first word and the hyphen (for the one who breaks the
relationship still cannot take the hyphen with him; the
lover naturally keeps the hyphen on his side)" (284).
Love is hardly a word, a thing, an object; it is more like a
hyphen, a dash that extends outward, capable of an infinite number of couplings, ever seeking completion.

Some of Kierkegaard's greatest exaggerations concern the concept of the neighbor, which does, as Adorno
and Outka suspect, occasionally threaten to become a
general and vapid category. This is not because Kierkegaard devalues the concrete needs of the other. On the
contrary, he moves from a very particular conception of
the neighbor—at one point he says that the neighbor is
simply any person who dwells near you, anybody you
meet—to a more general discourse about otherness precisely because of the stubborn demand that love include
everyone. Thus, what Adorno and Outka call abstraction
is really one key part of the process of Kierkegaard's
exaggeration.

> The concept of neighbor really means a duplicating
> of one's own self. Neighbor is what philosophers
> call the other, that by which the selfishness in self-
> love is to be tested. As far as thought is concerned
> the neighbor or other need not even exist. If a man
> living on a desert island formed his mind accord-
> ing to the command, he could by forsaking self-
> love be said to love his neighbor. (37)

This does sound as if the neighbor is reduced to an occasion for proving sacrificial love, a means to love understood as a solipsistic state rather than an allocentric action. However, a careful reading would uncover the true intention of Kierkegaard's remark. His image is really almost comical: a man living all alone, loving everybody but himself. The point is not to speculate about the nature of otherness or to treat the problem of love on a desert island as a philosophical conundrum. It does not matter who the neighbor is precisely because love is so expansive and so unbounded. The point is simply to love.

After all, finding the neighbor is not a difficult task: "Choosing a lover, finding a friend, yes, that is a long, hard job, but one's neighbor is easy to recognize, easy to find—if one will only recognize his duty" (39). Curiously, the more abstract and inflated the category of the neighbor becomes in this book, the more concrete the prohibition against preference. The highly abstract neighbor is easily deflated into the person, any person, you happen to meet. "There is in the whole world not a single person who can be received with such ease and certainty as one's neighbor. You can never confuse him with anyone else, for indeed all men are your neighbor" (64–5). Erotic love strains after the unique other who both extends and supplements the sense of self. Agape spreads out to encompass not the other in general, and certainly not that banal and fanciful category, the public—a category that Kierkegaard always hated because it refers to everybody and nobody, or rather reduces everybody to nobody—but simply any, or rather all individual others, without exception.

Although Adorno and Outka do not admit it, Kierkegaard does acknowledge the criticisms that will be raised against him. He knows that his conception of love will be accused of displacing friendship and eroticism. On this score he blames the "poet" for overpraising the wrong kinds of love. Poetic or pagan love is conditional, being based on feelings or various expectations (what

Outka would call mutuality). Christendom also exaggerates the possibilities of poetic love, lulling people into
hypocrisy. "The word Christendom as a common desig-
nation for a whole nation is a superscription which easily says too much and therefore easily leads the individual to believe too much about himself" (61). Christendom
is a shaky shelter, substituting comfort and security for
action and obedience. Only a love which has God, not
society, as a middle term, that is, which treats all people
equally, is a true love, transfigured by duty into the
eternal.

Christian talk about love, then, cannot be poetic. It
is not a matter of praising love. "Christianity is in itself
too profound, in its movements too serious for dancing
and skipping in such free-wheeling frivolity of talk
about the higher, the highest, the supremely highest"
(71). Christian love is more than the highest; it is
higher than that. It is the contradiction, the paradox,
the offense. Consequently, Kierkegaard denies that he
has been praising love. "Only in self-renunciation can a
man effectually praise love. No poet can do it" (335).
Metaphors elevate thought by creating unusual comparisons and driving rhetoric higher and higher into
increasingly refined insights and lyrical movements.
Hyperbole distances readers from their own self-understandings; it does not raise that understanding higher
by the use of vivid images, but rather threatens to
destroy that understanding with negations and exclamations that escape the bounds of reason.

Of course, hyperbole too can sound lyrical, as
Kierkegaard grudgingly and regretfully realized: "But I
am speaking almost as a poet!" (147). Ordinarily, however, religion and poetry are discontinuous because the
world fundamentally misunderstands the nature of
agape, or true love, and praises the wrong thing. Here
Kierkegaard anticipates Adorno's critique of the reduction of human relations to the process of exchange. The
world only understands love that is rewarded, that is
conserved. "The world is no better than this: the high-

est which it recognizes and loves, when it attains the
highest, is to love the good and mankind, and yet in
such a way that one also watches out for one's own and
a few others' earthly advantage" (127). At its best, sacrifice is practiced in the world only within the strict confines of the self-enclosed group. "What the world honours and loves under the name of love is group-
selfishness. The group also demands sacrifice and
devotion from the one whom it is to call loving" (123).
Indeed, the world calls the Christian selfish for holding
on to God, but it is only the inwardness of the God-rela-
tionship which can break the spell of exchange. True
sacrifice is not something that can be seen; it is not the
highest good, something that deserves praise. Such sacrifice is worldly; true sacrifice is not the highest but is
in fact invisible, wholly other.

Kierkegaard's obsession with inwardness, then, is
not the result of a metaphysics of subjectivism; moreover, it is not an attempt to deny the concrete reality of
the other. Rather, it is an attempt to root out of love all
thought of reward and admiration. Because of this subjectivism, this invisibility, Christian sacrifice cannot
really be explained or defended, and that troubles secularity. "The secular mind always needs to have decision
externalised; otherwise it mistrustfully believes that
the decision does not exist" (145). The value of that
which is not seen cannot be calculated and compared
and put into competition with other valuable acts. The
only way to resist the comparative mentality of secularity is to act as one unknown, to hide, to deceive.

Even more strange than its hiddenness, love violates
the dynamic of exchange by putting the lover into the
debt of the loved one. "This is the essential characteristic
of love: that the lover by giving infinitely comes into—
infinite debt" (172). The more you love, the more you
assume an insolvent debt. Love almost perversely puts
itself, not the other, into debt. This odd economy, or better, antieconomy of love is difficult to understand. Love,
like the French philosopher Georges Bataille's notion of

expenditure, recklessly departs from the law-like regular-
ity of recuperation and return by generously spending
more than common sense expectations require.[19] Kierkegaard would agree with Bataille that this capacity to
exceed expected modes of behavior endows humanity
with a distinctive and disruptive freedom, but whereas
Bataille sees expenditure as something that is natural,
almost organic, and something that results in waste, in
sacrifice without redemption, Kierkegaard's expenditure
runs counter to human instincts and is ultimately
directed toward life-affirming rather than life-denying
ends.

This antieconomy, which reverses the process of
exchange, cannot avoid leading to suffering for the lover,
the final stumbling block to secularity. "The purely
human conception of self-renunciation is this: give up
your selfish desires, longings and plans—and then you
will become appreciated and honoured and loved as a
righteous man and wise" (188). Agape is not an investment but a divestiture of the self in which love itself is
the only winner. "The world looks upon self-renunciation
only with shrewd practicality and therefore honours only
the self-renunciation which prudentially remains in
worldliness" (188). Love is an extravagant, a foolish giving which defies the laws of economics. "Love gives in
such a way that the gift appears as if it were the receiver's
possession" (255). Such giving is difficult because it
requires a double triumph: first the triumph of good over
evil, and then the triumph over this very triumph,
because true lovers never claim victory for themselves.

Adorno and Outka are correct to point out that this
discourse on sacrificial giving climaxes with a discussion of loving the dead. "In truth," Kierkegaard writes,
"if you really want to make sure about love in yourself
or in another person, then note how he relates himself
to one who is dead" (318). This is not necessarily the
greatest love, but it is the love in which one can be most
clear that true sacrifice is involved. There is no possibility of repayment here. The dead do not compel love.

This kind of love breaks the bondage of exchange. However, the dead are not the only ones who serve as a test case for love; the ugly serve a similar function. Kierkegaard resolutely separates love from any aesthetic considerations. To love the beautiful, which is, by definition, the object of desire and passion, is no great achievement. To love the ugly is much greater. "And what is the ugly? It is the neighbor, whom one shall love" (343). Kierkegaard's last word on love is not about the dead, but about the unlovable neighbor, all the people we do not feel inclined to like, or even look at, let alone love.

My analysis of love's hyperbole still leaves open the question of praxis, and perhaps it is the most difficult question for any hyperbolic discourse. What is the relationship between hyperbole and action? Is Adorno correct to suspect that at the end of the day Kierkegaard's discourse changes nothing? Would a more modest discourse, as Outka suggests, be more practically effective? Does hyperbole itself so stir the emotions that shock and resistance are more likely responses than action itself? Is hyperbole easily deflated into inactivity, into understatement?

Kierkegaard does frequently discuss the social implications of his position. His main point is that Christianity neither dissolves differences (including the difference between the rich and the poor) nor does it take sides. In fact, "Differences are like an enormous net in which the temporal is held" (82). This would seem to suggest that Adorno's suspicion of Kierkegaard's utopian tendencies is well founded: Kierkegaard's discourse is a dream that does not work, a laborless love. The politics of love hyperbolically construed, however, are more complex than that. It is important to note that Christianity does make the same demand on all, without exception. Christianity "allows all distinctions to stand, but it teaches the equality of the eternal" (82-3). Does this equality rise so far above ordinary existence, though, that in the end it does not

matter? Kierkegaard does sound at times very conservative in his attitude toward societal change. He suspects
that many people who preach against social distinctions are merely trying themselves to rise above those
distinctions. The enthusiasm of scholars and politi-
cians, he says, is not to be trusted. The cunning of criticism does not circumvent distinctions but increasingly
rationalizes them. What is needed is not more and better thinking but action itself.

The great gulf between thought and action is a
recurring theme in this book, and it is precisely this difference that Kierkegaard's discourse tries to overcome.
"It is one thing to let ideas strive with ideas; it is one
thing to battle and be victorious in a dispute; it is something else to be victorious over one's own mind when
one battles in the reality of life" (88). At the distance of
reflection, "one's neighbor is only a figment of the imagination...At a distance one's neighbor is a shadow which
in imagination enters every man's thought and walks
by" (89). People consistently confuse thought with
action. Christianity distrusts thought and demands
action, advocating equality without falling prey to the
easy temptations of self-righteousness and pride. As a
result, agape will be scorned by radicals and conserva-
tives alike. The hyperbole of agape will strike some as
too much and others as not enough. "But the equality of
eternity, to will to love one's neighbor, seems both too
little and too much, and therefore it is as if this love to
one's neighbor did not fit properly within the relationships of earthly existence" (90). Too little and too much:
This is at once the promise and the peril of hyperbole,
its strength and its weakness. Its demand invokes
denial. Understatement always lies near by.[20]

In sum, I have been trying to suggest that Kierkegaard's hyperboles are an attempt to derail thought into
action. He assumes that reflection and praxis are not on
a continuum but rather compete with one another.
Thought must turn against itself to make room for
action. The most extreme position on love denies all

reflection, rejects all questions and modifications, explanations and qualifications, in order to demand action. Hyperbole is always one step ahead of thought, quickly cutting it off from the escape of easy excuses. The commentaries of Outka and Adorno do raise pertinent questions, but precisely by raising reservations they tend to lead to more reflection, not action. Such analysis is important, especially concerning the relationship between sacrifice and mutuality and how that issue relates to feminist concerns. With love, though, it is sometimes appropriate, Kierkegaard is saying, to speak in another manner, to use a voice which does not invite speculation but demands action, to match style and substance in an explosive discourse that performs what it describes.

On these points Kierkegaard's discourse much resembles the thought of Emmanuel Levinas, whose discussion of the face of the other in terms of an infinite height also suggests that all reflection breaks down when ethical action is demanded.[21] The infinitude of the other cannot be represented by any reflective totality. One can only gaze at the face and acquiesce to the demand that we not kill. The imposition of the face breaks through all of our desires for control and reveals an ethical dimension that turns self-affirmation into self-donation. Levinas's heightened rhetoric functions in a similar way to Kierkegaard's—to make claims that cannot be conceptualized and to imagine a dimension that our desires normally conceal. Of course, there are differences between the two thinkers. Levinas operates within a strict phenomenological method that does not allow him to connect the infinity of the face with God or ethics with love.[22] Moreover, his philosophy is grounded in an analysis of otherness, intersubjectivity, while Kierkegaard is interested in a force, an exuberance whose demand originates outside of the domain of knowledge. However, both go to extremes to make what in the end is surely a simple point about the dignity and value of the life of the other.

When confronted with such hyperbole, one can only seek to defuse it—or act. In fact, Kierkegaard warns the reader not to be in too big of a hurry to say yes to love. It is better to say no and then to change one's mind than it is to say yes and then do nothing. The temptation of saying yes is an invitation to self-deception that hyperbole vigorously tries to resist. The way leading from no through repentance to the doing of good is shorter than the way that begins with yes and remains in reflection. This is Kierkegaard's not-so-hidden agenda: to make love impossible, to make you say no, but to haunt you with the possibility of saying yes. In fact, hyperbole by its very extremity does welcome criticisms and corrections, the commentaries of Outka and Adorno and countless others, but it also, by its very excess, reverberates and resonates throughout all such responses as a possibility which stubbornly persists. Indeed, *Works of Love* borders on the tedious because one can never say enough about love; that is precisely the point: one cannot say enough, but one can act.

Kierkegaard is always aware of his own strategy. "We have too earnest a conception of Christianity to entice anyone; we wish rather almost to give warning" (190). The ironic "almost" notwithstanding, this admission points to the difference between persuasion and provocation, demonstration and denunciation, metaphor and hyperbole. To talk about Christianity one cannot be moderate and careful, academic, as it were. "The more learned, the more excellent the defence, the more Christianity is disfigured, abolished, exhausted like an emasculated man, for the defence simply out of kindness will take the possibility of offence away" (193). A rhetoric of defense assumes continuity between the rhetorician and the audience as well as a certain detachment toward the subject matter. With some subjects, however, at some times, it is more important to shout than to organize reasonable discussions. Kierkegaard's distinctiveness is that he holds this always to be true about Christian love. "Essentially the truth must be regarded as polemic in

this world" (336). Anything less than hyperbole is compromise, accommodation, surrender—turning Christian
talk of love into a redundant echo of what the world
already knows. In sum, hyperbole is the work of love—
not a recreational distraction or a superfluous diversion
but a style that makes the impossible both practical and
necessary.

Kierkegaard is also realistic about the risk hyperbole involves. "But now when the world is proudly and
calmly self-assured of being Christian, the exaggeration
of a true Christian is worth no more than a laugh" (194).
The theologian, forced to exaggerate not only by the
uniform mediocrity, the understatement of Christendom, but also by the very nature of love itself, this ultimate exuberance, runs the risk of being taken for a
fool, of inciting scorn and derision, not understanding,
of appearing merely eccentric. Nevertheless, when
everybody assumes that Christianity has already triumphed, already spoken, and is therefore predictable
and mundane, the Christian gesture of love will be all
the more striking. It will draw attention to itself, just
like purple prose, but on closer examination it will
point away, to the mystery of God and the presence of
the neighbor.

Prose which stands out does risk looking ridiculous, not sublime. We all resent being the target of a joke
as much as we fear being deceived. Yet the best exaggerations do not isolate individuals or cause embarrassment but form a community; hyperboles (like laughter)
direct and discharge an enthusiasm that can break down
barriers by disclosing realities that transcend and thus
unite individual effort. Decentering the ordinary in a
horizon of limitless possibilities can draw together disparate standpoints onto an open plane of a passionate
and inclusive imagination. This is the wager of hyperbole when nothing else can be said. After all, "Love's element is infinitude, inexhaustibility, immeasurability"
(176). To talk about love as if it were anything else
would be to talk about something else. To risk the

ridiculous is the price of the sublime. To say too much is still not enough. To reach a conclusion on this topic in word or deed is to go on and on and on.

Chapter
Three

Sacrifice as Surplus:
Georges Bataille and the Economy of Excess
in Itself

So the world of religious things is a partially imaginary world, though only in its outward form, and one which therefore lends itself more readily to the free creations of the mind. Also, since the intellectual forces which serve to make it are intense and tumultuous, the unique task of expressing the real with the aid of appropriate symbols is not enough to occupy them. A surplus generally remains available which seeks to employ itself in supplementary and superfluous works of luxury, that is to say, in works of art. There are practices as well as beliefs of this sort. The state of effervescence in which the assembled worshippers find themselves must be translated outwardly by exuberant movements which are not easily subjected to too carefully defined ends. In part, they escape aimlessly, they spread themselves for the mere pleasure of so doing, and they take delight in all sorts of games. Besides in so far as the beings to whom the cult is addressed are imaginary, they are not able to contain and regulate this exuberance; the pressure of tangible and resisting realities is required to confine activities to exact and economical forms. Therefore one exposes oneself to grave misunderstandings if, in explaining rites, he believes that each gesture has a precise object and a definite reason for its existence. There are some which serve nothing; they merely answer the need felt by worshippers for action, motion, gesticulation. They are to be seen jumping, whirling, dancing, cry-

59

ing and singing, though it may not always be possible to give a meaning to all this agitation. Therefore religion would not be itself if it did not give some place to the free combinations of thought and activity, to play, to art, to all that recreates the spirit that has been fatigued by the too great slavishness of daily work: the very same causes which called it into existence make it necessary.

—Emile Durkheim,
The Elementary Forms of the Religious Life

The superfluous is very necessary.

Voltaire, *Le Mondain*

Could it be that religion, driven from the center of life by the hostile forces of science and secularism, has properly found its home at the margins? Does religion, shorn of all utility, stripped of its metaphysics and moralities, still illuminate the key dynamic structure of human being? For Georges Bataille,[1] religion, above and beyond all of its idiosyncracies, expresses a pure feeling, a fundamental attitude, that makes life meaningful: only in an absolute giving, an expenditure that knows no boundaries, categories, or restriction, an abundant divestiture of the self that is reckless in its disregard for custom or calculation, can life affirm itself. For Bataille, excess is the basic word that defines humanity, and he equates excess with sacrifice, a giving that reveals glory through destruction. Sacrifice, however, is an expenditure that is not inscribed within a system of redemption. Religion is turned against itself to liberate from worn moral codes the power of liberation itself, the ability to give. Sin is avarice, and grace is the gratuitous nature of giving. Excess, hyperbole vivified, is the act that constitutes human freedom by bowing to no interplay of reward and punishment, no limitations of good and evil. Excess as sacrifice, sublimely superfluous, is inaugurated against the very promises and prohibitions that make redemption possible.

An overflowing of the will reminiscent of the laughter of Nietzsche's overman, Bataille's excess arises more from strength than weakness.[2] It is the illogical defiance of the practical laws of survival, the tedious rules of sociability, and the moderate principles of ethical restraint. Bataille's genius is to see that at every moment we can always cut across expectations, upset conventions, overcome hesitations. Freedom is defined as transgression and not transcendence; to give is always to go against. Every expenditure is a denial—of a reward, an expectation, a hope or plan. To spend is to become undone, to waste ruthlessly, arrogantly, against all reasonable reservations. Excess is the last hope of a humanity mired in a cautious and timid rationalism, a *homo oeconomicus* trained to act in terms of cost benefit analysis, investment, and return. Sacrifice is a surplus value, a remainder, a waste that survives the economy of exchange, where interaction is governed by the exhaustive utilization of every production. Excess is luxury: the little explosion that says who we are by denying what we are supposed to be.[3]

A sovereign expenditure of this magnitude is neither a task nor a burden; it is a jubilation, an inebriated blurring of boundaries that entails its own risk and excitement. Against Kierkegaard's subordination of hyperbole to ethics in the infinite discourse of love, Bataille locates excess in the festival, the orgy, the frenzied ritual of a bloody sacrifice, and above all mystical anguish, where the self does not find fulfillment by obeying the universal laws of the ethical or by putting the other first in all considerations but by violently losing itself altogether. The festival that Bataille imagines, however, is not a celebration where people come together in a sacred space to step out of time, disrupting ordinary boundaries in order to merge with the greater being of the whole community, thus finding the fullness of time itself. Rather, Bataille's many celebrations of excess constitute a discourse of loss, of agony and mourning.[4] Expenditure is an antisocial movement across the abyss of freedom, at best a guilty pleasure and more likely a solitary reenactment of death. Excess plays between feast and funeral in a game that transacts both exuberant displays of giving and the ultimate crossing of final limits.

Bataille is trying to do justice to a phenomenon that is, by definition, out of (our) control; more to the point, Bataille embodies an excess that itself seeks some kind of understanding. In Bataille we hear hyperbole striving for articulation, and it is a hyperbole that has become the hyperbolic, a shocking force that we cannot comprehend but to which we can submit. The basic claim is that excess *in itself*, grasped essentially, is *for itself*, disconnected from any goal or object. Kierkegaard's compassion for the other is conspicuously missing here, making me suspect that there is an absence in Bataille's discourse that demands interrogation. Indeed, it is crucial to distinguish in Bataille a commentary on the aimlessness of excess and the suggestion that excess aims at nothing and then to ask what makes that nothingness so powerful and seductive. I will insist in pursuing how Bataille frames and uses the hyperbolic, in order to wager that excess unfettered and aimless actually has limits and a purpose and to prepare the way for a very different reading of the violence of hyperbole in Flannery O'Connor.

Bataille approaches excess in many different and not always coherent ways, perhaps most successfully through his viciously erotic and perversely cunning novels and stories.[5] Even in his nonfiction work, however, Bataille is always dramatizing excess to enact its power to seduce and (mis)lead us from everyday routines into theatrically charged moments of revelatory disorientation. His experiments with style and genre are essential to his project, as Derrida discerns:

> How, after having exhausted the discourse of philosophy, can one inscribe in the lexicon and syntax of a language, our language, which was also the language of philosophy, that which nevertheless exceeds the

oppositions of concepts governed by this communal logic? Necessary and impossible, this excess had to fold discourse into strange shapes.[6]

Derrida is skeptical of Bataille's attempt to displace the drive for system and closure in philosophy with the unpredictable openness and lack of reserve of erotic literature. Derrida is interested in Bataille as an example of a kind of writing that self-destructively tries to escape the provenance of metaphysics, a task that for Derrida himself is both necessary and impossible. It is not necessary, however, to analyze the stories and novels to locate Bataille's rebellion against philosophical restraint and moderation; his theoretical works exhibit and manipulate the tension between articulation (clarity, concision, circumspection) and something unspeakably other, the expression of an ecstatic trance that seeks to unravel the text of philosophy by immodestly pointing to the something more that reason can never know. Bataille's system, to the extent that he has one, is torn, perforated, leaky; it includes many positions, opinions, agendas, but it always lets everything—carelessly and irresponsibly—escape.

I will focus on Bataille's more theoretical works, following excess through several thematics and across various domains: from an exploration of inner experience, the mystical unsayable, to reflections on the equally unspeakable vulgarity of excrement and the category of the obscene; from a theory of transgression, which includes an erotics and an incipient theology, to a systematic bio-economics and finally to a fully developed theory of religion. In all of these somewhat disjointed and scattered moves, Bataille oscillates between two opposed methods, two different styles. On the one hand, his talk about waste, orgies, destruction, and disconnected body parts is meant to defeat and dissipate the usual expectations, standards, and values of rigorous thinking and decent living. Hyperbole is dangerous, upsetting, strange, not just lacking in taste but literally distasteful. On the other hand, Bataille also seeks to explain excess, to give it a voice, even to personify it, and he connects it at various times to biology, economics, philosophy, and religion. Excess is exploited as part of a system; it is neutralized as an aspect of nature. It is defended as reasonable, and it is returned, finally, to its origin in religion. Certainly excess is too much to enclose within any single vocabulary, but it is important to trace throughout Bataille's discourses a need to make sense of excess, to place it in a context, to render it fathomable, even useful. Caught in the middle of this tension is a dissonant movement that exceeds and upsets language itself, and thus a force whose direction it is crucial, if possible, to ascertain. I will argue not only that Bataille finally does give excess an object, a referent, but also that this object or goal must be different from what Bataille ultimately imagines.

All of Bataille's interests in excess can be found in the two chief works of his *La Somme athéologique, Inner Experience* (1943), and *Guilty* (published in 1944 but begun in 1939), where they are articulated as an aspect of an experience that is simultaneously silent and assertive, painful and exhilarating, hidden and violent.[7] Both texts—hardly mentioning the Second World War but expressing a futile rage that presupposes a constant awareness of the historical context—constitute an ambitious attempt to displace Jewish and Christian mysticism with an experience of an interiorized beyond, a condensed event in which the self finds a total and unbounded release that renders discourse and rationality impotent. Bataille draws upon not only his education in a seminary (he converted to Roman Catholicism in 1914) but also a period of profound mysticism spent in 1922 at a Benedictine abbey on the Isle of Wight (he renounced his faith soon afterwards). These early religious experiences are filtered through a melancholy sense of the loss of God, creating a religiously tinged passion that is bereft of any object.

The play of two radically different metaphors,

especially alternated in *Inner Experience*, reveal the confusion of this a-theological act: it both strives for the summit and loses itself in the labyrinth. Summit and labyrinth are recurring, juxtaposed images that are meant to show the simultaneous thrill and frustration of excess, which is a desire to become everything (a basic denial of human finitude) that is constantly qualified by the thought of death (the ultimate expression of that finitude). "As I approached the summit," Bataille teases in *Guilty*, "everything got confused. At the decisive moment there's always something else to do" (*G*, 97). What dares this summit-turned-labyrinth is an overwhelming passion of uncertain origins that is capable of tearing through the self and creating new visions out of the fragmentary ruins of the ensuing explosion.

Neither of these books is written in a systematic manner. Instead, aphorisms, anecdotes, absurd scribbles and poetic convulsions depict the drama of the self in which knowledge is as unacceptable as salvation. "I write for one," Bataille explains, "who entering into my book, would fall into it as into a hole, who would never again get out" (*IE*, 116). Nothing is promised, and uncertainty is confronted by a desperate and delirious courage. "I remain in intolerable non-knowledge, which has no other way out than ecstasy itself" (*IE*, 12). The ruptured/raptured self not only cannot be described but also cannot speak. Words are treacherous, slippery. Bataille is reduced to paradox, nonsense, irreverence. "I have of the divine an experience so mad that one will laugh at me if I speak of it" (*IE*, 33). Through facing the impossible the self tries to transform anguish into delight. By both willing and denying literally everything, the self transgresses all boundaries and begins a fall that is both dizzying and enthralling.

Only at the extreme limit, where excess rebounds from the impossible and yet refuses to acknowledge any boundaries, does life overcome impotence and degradation. At times, Bataille's descriptions of this limit are banal, mired in abstract and vague terms.[8] He is most moving when he tries to portray the fundamentally inaccessible vertigo of falling that freedom shorn of salvation evokes but does not directly speak. Freedom as sacrifice is a madness, a renunciation of knowledge, where "nothing, neither in the fall nor in the void, is revealed, for the revelation of the void is but a means of falling further into absence" (*IE*, 51–2). In passages like this the reader becomes aware that Bataille is trying to delimit the boundaries of a fog. Other comments are more easily grasped. "Existence is a tumult which overflows, wherein fever and rupture are linked to intoxication" (*IE*, 81). Excess is the displacement of subjectivity that neither regrets nor resists its replacement in the ordinary that it has violated and overcome. Systematic expostulation is impossible; philosophy cannot explain, that is, make a profit from the loss of excess. Bataille nevertheless hastens to caress and probe the dispossession that is the height of subjectivity, vainly striving to correlate language and event.

In this struggle to articulate the purely subjective, religious terminology persists with a rigor that is odd for a devoted Nietzschean. Bataille is especially dependent on the concept of sacrifice, a term that denoted for Nietzsche the false humility of Christian pride, a cover for the resentment of the weak.[9] For Bataille, as he clearly states in *Guilty*, sacrifice still has redemptive powers in a post-theistic culture: "Sacrifice will illuminate the conclusion of history as it did its dawn" (*G*, 51). Bataille wants to return to the classical arguments against the propriety of sacrifice—as diverse as Plato and the Hebrew prophets—and almost spitefully appropriate it for just those very reasons: sacrifice *is* senseless, bloody, shocking, not worthy of the noble or reflective or moral person. An almost demonic divestiture of the self, sacrifice is the last vestige of freedom. By closely approximating destruction and death while also assigning to the sacrificer a certain measure of invulnerability and mastery, it comically reenacts that which can only be experienced where all experience ceases.[10]

Bataille does not conceive of sacrifice as an attempt to transfer the burden of one's own subjectivity onto somebody else; it is also not a project, in the sense of a moral act of compassion and giving. Indeed, he regrets the spiritualization or sublimation of sacrifice in Christianity, where the dramatic and the awesome act of a bloody ritual becomes moralized and personalized as a basic duty, even generalized as the structure of authentic subjectivity, and thus deprived of its peril. In Bataille's vision of sacrifice primitive and modern elements are oddly mixed. "Assuredly, this word sacrifice signifies this: that men, by virtue of their will, introduce certain goods into a dangerous region, where destructive forces prevail" (*IE*, 96). He is clearly not talking about animal sacrifices, whether they are for expiation, aversion, communion, or tribute. Nor is he talking about sacrifice as the subjective expression of obedience to a love ethic. Instead, sacrifice is a destructive act—which culminates when it is turned inward, against the self—from which nothing arises but upon which everything is at stake.

> Sacrifice can't be for us what it was at the beginning of "time." Our experience is one of impossible appeasement. Lucid holiness recognizes in itself the need to destroy, the necessity for a tragic outcome. (*G*, 51)

In sacrifice lies the mystery of the creativity of destruction.[11]

A godless, pointless, and yet fundamentally sacramental sacrifice is a long way from Nietzsche. Bataille replaces the vitriolic polemic of Nietzsche's "God is dead" with a sensual embrace of the subsequent nothingness. He sees that the absence of God does not mean the irrelevance and dissolution of religion. Instead, religion is denied its object, but by that very restriction religion returns to a more primordial scene. The longing of religion, especially of mystics and their negative theologies, the anguish and despair, the celebration of suffering and the violence of the sacred, all of these components are carefully reconstituted around the absence of an ultimate object. Here is Zarathustra's overcoming without the strained bravado, the forced confidence, the oblique hints of a metaphysics of the will and an eternal return, the arrogant and thus insecure rhetoric of the warrior, the hyperbole of the prophet. Here is a self-overcoming that is painful, incomplete, ugly and, in the end, silent. Zarathustra has been broken by the absence of God.

The confessional *Guilty* advances many of these themes in a haphazard but poetic way; it is thus both more concrete and more oblique than *Inner Experience.* "I intend a description of mystical experience," he states, "and am apparently off the track, but in the confusion I introduce, what track could there be?" (*G*, 19). The track he does increasingly follow is the mingling of eroticism and mysticism in his explication of the basic human need for ruin. The cracks in human existence, those spaces through which we squeeze against all constraints into emptiness, are the glory of humanity. Freedom is a wound that cannot be healed. In fact, Bataille finds ecstasy not in eroticism understood as pleasure but in imagining himself being tormented. The *Alleluia, The Catechism of Dianus,* appended to *Guilty,* confirms Bataille's disdain for a pleasure that satisfies: "The only pleasure worth desiring is the desire for pleasure and not pleasure" (*G*, 147). Desire unbound—"Doesn't an always unfinished universe yawn between your legs?"— masochistically seeks not some goal or closure but those possibilities that are impossible and therefore necessary obstacles for the exercise of freedom.

These reflections on the erotic lead Bataille to two other obscenities, chance and laughter. Chance is celebrated as a phenomenon that reason cannot grasp. It rudely resists all calculations, yet it is as seductive and as fascinating as a catastrophe. Chance is a marginal experience that takes us to where "The course of things escapes us at the extremes" (G, 71). Submission to chance encourages a playful but violent loss of self-control. It is, in the end, Bataille's experience of grace. "I can't imagine a spiritual way of life that isn't impersonal, dependent on chance, never on efforts of the will" (G, 74). Chance liberates our power to deny all of the plans and goals and agendas we have for ourselves. "Chance is a state of grace, a gift of heaven, permission to roll the dice, without any possibility of repetition, without anguish" (G, 78). Laughter is a similarly disorienting event; it is a violent discharge that puts us at odds with the world. We laugh because the world does not make sense, and yet we release ourselves into the nonsense. "Laughter hangs suspended, it doesn't affirm anything, doesn't assuage anything" (G, 101). The gape of laughter displays the wound of freedom without asking to be healed.

Religion surfaces in bits and pieces in *Guilty*, both as a repression and a manifestation of excess. God, for Bataille, is basically a confusion of the sacred and reason, an attempt to rationalize and objectify the mystery of sacrifice—a safety net. Bataille also argues that belief in God is based on the need to imagine a solid, stable self, a self without excess.

> I don't believe in God—from inability to believe in self. Belief in God is belief in self. God is only a guarantee given to me. If we didn't project the self on the absolute we'd be convulsed with laughter. (G, 45)

For the religious person, it is tempting to imagine God as a boundary, as the being who gives each being its own place. The absence of God blurs all boundaries and makes excess inevitable. God's absence is infinite, and humanity's experience of this nothingness has a sacred character. "God isn't humanity's limit-point, though humanity's limit-point is divine. Or put it this way— humanity is divine when experiencing limits" (G, 105).

Transgression, sacrifice, entering the presence of God's absence, is a sacred but hardly a comforting or peaceful event. "God is dead. He's so dead, in fact, that the only way to make this comprehensible is by killing myself" (*G*, 85). Only ultimate acts of destruction can affirm the void that opens in God's absence, an absence that is the staggering and disorienting summit of human experience.

Philosophy, language, reason all fail as spectacularly as religion to grasp the inner experience of excess. Of course, the a-rational is indescribable: "The absence of a solution cannot be expressed" (*G*, 21). Excess, however, is more than just an impossible puzzle. Once we venture to understand it we can no longer imagine what it might be like to feel it, and we cannot simply will it to happen. In the middle of *Guilty* Bataille desperately recognizes his dilemma, and he laments his own desire for communication and explanation. Above all, he regrets his inability to lose control. "Even in me as I write, the work of understanding continues. I'm condemned at least to know what I'm saying. Short of death, there's no way for me to lose myself in this night" (*G*, 66).[12] Despair is the paralyzing confusion of the desire to lose everything when desire itself drives us toward consummation, toward gain. Despair, however—as with Kierkegaard's sickness unto death—can lead to answers if we embrace it with abandon. "What I call night is different from the darkness of thought—night has the violence of light" (*G*, 108). Night can be so stunningly bright that it can blind us with its truth if we stare too long.

The daring sensuality of the mystery of sacrifice is the focus of *Erotism* (*L'Erotisme*, 1957), where Bataille draws on his early interests in surrealism, the Marquis de Sade, and theology to synthesize eroticism, death, and mysticism in a theory of intimacy and transgression.[13] Two experiences are pivotal: 'giving up', negative acts of surrender and denial, and the sacramental character of the dissolution of the self. Bataille was always interested in the grotesque, the crudely material, even the despicable and intolerable as symbols of the unrestricted and unconventional aspects of excess. In this book the vulgar and coarse aspects of eroticism come to the foreground to represent all those acts in which the self exercises its destructive potential not only to violently reject ordinary boundaries and limitations but also to establish a sense of oneness and wholeness. Eroticism reveals to separate beings "their fundamental continuity, like the waves of a stormy sea" (E, 22). Acts of excess arise from a nostalgic longing for a lost intimacy (like Freud's oceanic feeling[14]) that is the emblem of the leveling power of the sea of death; erotic acts lead us across this great expanse, reeling back from the point of no return, where the world ends and everything disappears, sinking into the void.

The unity of desire and violence is dramatized on the body. The violation of the boundaries of the body, which signify the rules and constraints that always keep life organized and ordered, is the key to Bataille's understanding of eroticism. It is also the deepest expression and the most basic configuration of a desire for intimacy that necessarily takes the shape of aggression, because the displacement of the self is always experienced as the opening of a wound. Moreover, the sacrificial loss of the self, taken too far, inevitably leads to death. The erotic act opens onto a space that is literally nowhere. Eroticism is thus the search for a oneness that everybody desires but that is, in the end, vacant of any coherent meaning. The desperation of this drive determines the lack of balance and mutuality in Bataille's conception of the erotic. In terms of intersubjectivity, the other for Bataille can only represent an opportunity for mastery or resignation. Although he privileges submission over domination, one presupposes the other, and in either case, transgressions of bodily order lead to an ecstatic blurring of self-other borders in which the tensions that define the self are relaxed and exhausted, leaving the self emptied and undone. Excitement and pleasure are gained through a risk of abandonment that can never be fully consum-

mated. Once spent, the self must begin this reenactment of the drive to the void all over again if, paradoxically, the self is to remain a separate entity. In love we
flirt with death by becoming masters of our capacity for
submission.[15]

Fundamental to this account of eroticism is the
claim that discontinuity constitutes the normal state of
affairs. However, discontinuity, the everyday separation
of all beings, is not natural or given; it is a cultural
achievement sustained and enforced by the need for
work, for labor. In other texts economics will replace
eroticism as the key organizational term for excessive
impulses. Here Bataille is interested in labor only due to
its institution of rules and laws—taboos—that set up
the limitations that make productivity possible. Prohibitions are the preconditions not only for useful activity but for thought and science, every form of lucidity.
Taboos are not absolute, however; they invoke duplici-
tous ambivalence rather than require perfect obedience. The taboo is, in a way, created by its violation;
transgression causes the guilt and reverence without
which the taboo could not properly function. Taboos do
not simply combat violence; they also incite it. Perversely, in this secret marriage of heaven and hell, one
is not possible without the other.

Most taboos, Bataille notes, are directed against
sexual impulses and the violence of death. Burial rites,
the prohibition against murder, and the regulations of
sexual activity all serve to demarcate the boundaries of
a productive discontinuity. During sacred periods the
profane space of work is punctuated by festivals that
permit and even encourage activities that break the
laws. Along with feast days and ritual festivals, orgies
are also merely a symptom of the fascination of the forbidden. "It [the orgy] is a religious effusion first and
foremost; it is essentially the disorder of lost beings
who oppose no further resistance to the frantic proliferation of life" (E, 113). The taboo represses and redirects
a desire that nonetheless asserts itself and finds in its

violations a guilty, inner pleasure. Michel Foucault bril-
liantly summarizes this insight: "It is likely that transgression has its entire space in the line it crosses."[16]
The establishment of limits is at once their denial, an
oscillation of creation and destruction, "a spiral which
no simple infraction can exhaust."[17] Transgression is
neither unethical nor amoral; its violence sustains that
against which it is empowered.

Christianity does not recognize these pagan ambiguities.[18] It rejects "the desire to use violent means to
probe the secrets of existence" (*E*, 91). Religion is the
original domain of Bacchic violence, but Christianity
opposes transcendence to transgression and forbids
organized celebrations of transgression. Bataille basically has a dualistic, even Manichaean interpretation of
Christianity; he accuses it of totally separating good
and evil, purifying the divine of violence and the believers of sin. Christianity rejects impurity; excess is
degraded as immoral by a system that substitutes obedience for temptation.[19] The devil is driven out of
heaven, destroying the creativity of profanation. Good
and evil are polarized as absolute opposites (evil is a
present and oppressive reality framed by the good at
both ends: nostalgia for pure, prelapsarian origins and
dreams of utopian endings) instead of being joined as
relational and relative pairs. Sacrifice is rationalized as
God's act of self-reconciliation, not the empowering disorientation of finite creatures foolishly seeking the infinite. Indeed, Christianity misunderstands humanity's
impossible need for continuity by inventing an infinite
discontinuity, "a discontinuity unassailable by death"
(*E*, 119)—the immortality of discontinuous beings. God
thus preserves discontinuity rather than demands
futile acts of continuity.

Bataille actually regrets the decline of belief in the
devil. Christianity first objectifies evil, then disconnects it from the good, and with the rise of liberalism
and rationalism evil is ignored and forgotten altogether.
By dividing the kingdom of God from the kingdom of

humanity, Christianity risks destroying both realms. The power of evil is lost, especially its power to create the sacred. Since eroticism is no longer a sin, eroticism itself begins to fade. "In an entirely profane world nothing would be left but the animal mechanism. No doubt the memory of sin might persist; it would be like feeling that there was a trap somewhere!" (*E*, 128). Freud was wrong to think that civilization creates only the discontent; it also provides for forbidden pleasures that are not possible in a culture where everything is allowed. With the decline of taboos, however, one must work all the harder to find acts worthy of transgression. In our increasingly permissive culture, acts of transgression become surreptitious and furtive, dislocated from the public to the private realm. This explains Bataille's interest in the obscene and the disgusting; only extreme and secretive categories funded by the common and clandestine experience of sex can provide for excessive acts in a liberal age.

In his fiction Bataille vividly portrays the disturbing and startling confrontation of the ordinary with the obscene, finding in sensuality a dramatic struggle in which the self tries to but never quite succeeds in losing itself. Bataille also attempts to systematize his fascination with the vulgar and the distasteful in such concepts as heterology, a neologism he invented to oppose the reign of homogeneity, the rule of the similar or the same. He often writes about the bestiality of human behavior, the human filth that civilization does its best to hide, the fascination the intolerable holds upon us. Bataille is working against prejudices that serve to denigrate experiences that are not susceptible to rational illumination. "The heterogeneous asserts a 'base' materialism exhibiting intractable, unsubmissive forces."[20] The repugnant or the ugly arrests thought, inhibits our demand that all objects be useful, and forces us to imagine a superfluous dimension that slips free from the domain of utility.

Bataille's materialism is not amenable to scientific

or Marxist analysis; it is, however, a movement toward an explanation, a philosophical placement of excess. In fact, at times it seems that he is merely reversing the Platonic or idealist hierarchy that separates the "high" from the "low": Bataille accepts the distinction but chooses the bottom of the scale. His project, however, is not really metaphysical: "Low can be a concept no more than it can be part of a project."[21] Trash can be recycled into usable products only with great difficulty. "Heterology," Denis Hollier explains, "would be the theory of that which theory expels."[22] To imagine the ugly and repulsive, no matter how systematically, is to take thought to the brink of disaster where the other remains unretrievably different. Bataille wants to lower thought, to deal it low blows, in order to interrupt the sway of reason. He wants to stand reason on its (decapitated) head by beginning with the bottom, exposing the underside that thought tries to purify and conceal. Sacrifice as excess is a wild gesture that is, in the end, indistinguishable from excretion: a discharge that is as unworthy of evaluation as it is necessary, a release that disgusts as it relieves.

The paradox of heterology is not meant to be a systematic or metaphysical contextualization of excess; however, it does show how Bataille strains toward grand theories and new vocabularies in order to explain the unexplainable. Bataille is never sure, it seems—and the uncertainty accounts for his stylistic brilliance—if excess is aimless or if it has an object, a goal, a purpose. For example, alongside the discourse on the delirium of mysticism and eroticism, and never synthesized with it, Bataille sought a divergent path to the summit of excess that would (re)place the unsayable and unthinkable (with)in the context of economics and biology. The key concepts and categories of this more scientific route to excess are developed in a crucial essay published in 1933, "The Notion of Expenditure" ("La Notion de depénse").[23] Here he posits the idea of unproductive expenditure, or what he calls in a letter to Alexandre

Kojève "unemployed negativity" (*G*, 123). What humanity needs is a negativity that is recognized and experienced but nevertheless unutilized, wasted: a negativity
without content.[24] The environment of excess thus
shifts from the subjective to the economic, from experience to labor; Bataille succeeds in burying excess in a
morass of speculative economic and anthropological
theories. Humanity recognizes, he argues, the right to
acquire and the need to consume; modern economies
are based on the moderate pleasures of production and
conservation. Pleasure is a concession or diversion to
work. What modern economies do not recognize is the
importance of the need to spend unproductively, violating laws of interest and utility. Excess is thus linked to
an economy, or better, an antieconomy, that threatens to
burst through the stable systems of supply and
demand, of exchange, that today regulate and channel
our desires.

Bataille borrows much of his analysis of economics
from a famous study by Marcel Mauss, *The Gift*, an
attempt to show that the ritualized act of presenting
gifts constitutes a rudimentary economy from which
more complex systems of exchange developed.[25] Giving
in primal cultures, according to Mauss, is a highly sym-
bolic activity governed by many rules and regulations;
it is both an expression of a loss but also the creation of
a debt, an obligation. Primal cultures—and Mauss is
especially interested in the potlatch rituals of the Indi-
ans of North America, developing an analysis that
Bataille often repeats—require a three-fold logic of giving, receiving, and repaying in order to insure social
bonds. Giving does more than redistribute wealth and
goods; it creates communion and alliance because the
gift is always valued as symbolically a part of the giver.
In some cultures, the power to spend establishes social
prestige that can arouse rivalry and even violence.
Mauss approaches what he calls the religious origins of
economics with nostalgia and expectation. Today we
see gift giving as a marginal, incidental, private activ-

ity; against the triumph of acquisitive mercantilism Mauss wants to return to the ritualized customs of giving to replace the utilitarianism of modern notions of exchange and to humanize the impersonal demands of the market.[26]

Breaking with Mauss's sentimental attitude but drawing on much of his research, Bataille seeks in giving not reform but revolution. For Bataille, the fact that giving, not bartering—donations that are excessive and thus humiliate and obligate the donee—is at the root of exchange opens up a completely new way of thinking about economics. The gift is not only a challenge; it is a destructive act for its own sake. Bataille has shifted the accent on giving from reciprocity to loss. "It is through loss that glory and honor are linked to wealth" (*VE*, 122). People accumulate fortunes not for a shelter from need but in order to expedite a limitless loss. True, in modern culture orgiastic generosity has all but disappeared. Like Mauss, Bataille wants to return to primal economic models, but his goal is not to modify market economies but to replace them with a way of acting that radically threatens the notion of exchange powered by consumption.

Loss, not need or desire, becomes for Bataille a fundamental aspect of human nature, of human expression. Not conspicuous consumption (Thorstein Veblin) but audacious expenditure is the privilege of the wealthy, the strong. Bataille rejects the Marxist demand for total utility, a distribution of goods that would be radically rational and humane. In gambling, sacrifice, eroticism, war, even in Christ's death, a form of giving can be glimpsed that has the power to disrupt all attempts to rationalize exchange. "In each case the accent is placed on a loss that must be as great as possible in order for that activity to take on its true meaning" (*VE*, 118). Production is subordinated to destruction; the desire for gain disguises the deeper and more basic longing for loss.

For Mauss, loss serves the Durkheimian function of

social solidarity and cohesion. For Bataille, loss means upheaval, anarchy. Nevertheless, he does connect loss to a general theory of political economy, thus treating it as functional and useful. This theory is most clearly presented in *The Accursed Share* (*La Part maudite*, 1949), a speculative explanation of the role loss plays in a global and ultimately biological theory of socialization.[27] Habermas calls this a "metaphysical (in the pejorative sense) worldview."[28] Even here, though, writing, explanation, and communication are problematic. This is a book, Bataille admits, that he could "not have written if he had followed its lessons to the letter" (*AS*, 11). Excess escapes the system that he nevertheless self-destructively struggles to elaborate.

Bataille's ambition is great. He does not treat economics as an isolated, abstract set of models or theories. He places production and consumption in a larger framework, in the context of the movements of energy spread throughout every level of existence on the entire globe. Bataille treats it as a basic fact that living organisms receive more energy than they need for the maintenance of life. This excess of energy, wealth, can be utilized for the growth of the life system, but when that system reaches its growth limits, excess can no longer be absorbed and therefore must be lost without any profit or return. "It must be spent, willingly or not, gloriously or catastrophically" (*AS*, 21). Life is like a crowd that cannot fit into a stadium, rendering violence necessary.

Surplus, not scarcity, is thus the foundation of economics. Profit is only apparently accumulated for further investment; its secret aim is waste. Saving is not a limitless activity; it has a logic that defies the limitations of usefulness. Bataille is aware that modern economies try to work against this basic human drive— economies are structures that organize the repression of expenditure—but the archaic sensibility still persists as a protest against the bourgeois mind. Bataille admires the Aztecs who "were just as concerned about sacrificing as we are about work" (*AS*, 46), and he argues that they went to war not for conquest but for a spectacular expenditure. It is no accident, Bataille suggests, that wars coincide with a general rise in standards of living. The Aztecs also went to war to find more victims for sacrifices, a ritual they understood well: in this event both the sacrificer and the victim experience the intimacy of the liberating power of an act that defies the laws of labor. Destruction serves to negate the otherwise oppressively strong domination of utility.

Bataille slips easily from economics and biology to world history and prophecy. The wealthy, he suggests, have abdicated their traditional roles of expenditure and loss. Modern cultures have lost the capacity for splendor and spectacle. Society no longer sanctions great public acts of destruction. We increase our resources without any sense of where this might lead us. Bataille is especially critical of Soviet communism, which is an immense machine blinded to the reality of nonproductive activity. Capitalist economies have more potential for excess, he argues, although the bourgeois mind still subordinates expenditure to production. The real problem, though, does not lie with historical shifts or economic organizations; excess is a fundamentally insoluble act. "How can man find himself—or regain himself—seeing that the action to which the search commits him in one way or another is precisely what estranges him from himself?" (*AS*, 131). All attempts to explain or organize excess must inevitably fail: the moment of pure expenditure is self-conscious only when consciousness is not of something but has nothing as its object.

These tangled lines of thought find their most systematic presentation in Bataille's *Theory of Religion* (1948).[29] Religion is, after all, the most primary expression of excess as well as its most sophisticated organization and explanation. In *The Accursed Share* Bataille defines religion as "the satisfaction that a society gives to the use of excess resources, or rather to their destruction (at least insofar as they are useful)" (*AS*, 12). Religion is the collective reaction to excess, an attempt to mediate its disruptive powers by absorbing and rationalizing it, making excess productive and acceptable. Religion, though, has not always served to defuse and contain that which drives us beyond. Indeed, the Reformation marks for Bataille the origin of the fundmantal mistake of modernity: it destroyed the mixture of the sacred and the profane by handing earth over to the men of production, the bourgeoisie.[30] The precarious balance of the ordinary and the outrageous was toppled.

Bataille's theory of religion reads like a reversal of Hegel's dialectic. The history of negation is not subsumed by ever widening circles of understanding and explanation; instead, excess stubbornly resists every synthesis and mediation. Excess originates at a transitional point in human evolution that does not allow it to develop and change: the immediacy of animal life recognizes no discontinuty between beings, treating destruction as natural, whereas the invention of tools forces humans to think in terms of utility, thus interrupting the continuity of existence with the demands of purposeful activity. Given the restraints of social stability, continuity can only be momentarily glimpsed through violent, wasteful acts. "Intimacy cannot be expressed discursively" (*TR*, 50). Sacrifice is a relinquishment, the antithesis of production, where something is consumed with only the moment in mind, but once reflection or self-consciousness begins, the logic of sacrifice is lost or misunderstood.

Because society produces a state of affairs that is essentially disturbing and unsatisfying, religion becomes both necessary and impossible. The divine is dangerous, even contagious; we are tempted to surrender wholeheartedly to continuity, but we hesitate, knowing that it would mean our death. "The sacred is exactly comparable to the flame that destroys the wood by consuming it" (*TR*, 53). The sacred festival offers only a partial solution to our dilemma: we desire intimacy, but prudently resist a return to an animal-like state of nondifferentiation. By entering into society, humans reject who they really are and doom themselves to frustration. Religion tries to find an answer to this problem, but it offers a search for lost intimacy that is bound to fail: continuity can never become the object of a project, a plan. Indeed, in modern culture sacrifice has lost its power by diverting attention from the violent release of the sacrificial act to the establishment of an order of sacred objects.

Religion falls prey to the reign of utility, diverting excess back into channels of productivity. Salvation is gained through a calculative act, and God is reduced to one thing among many other things. In fact, all areas of culture fall to the same fate of Weberian rationalization. Industrialization regulates the economy and thus severs it from its primordial purposes. Even the military order becomes increasingly planned and organized. War becomes methodical, and limits are placed on its wastefulness. Science too contributes to the lust for sense and order. The result is a tyranny of utility in which Bataille finds an apocalyptic dimension. "The intimate order is represented only through prolonged stammerings," he complains (*TR*, 96). History is the story of the increasing repression of excess, and Bataille wonders if some ultimate and perhaps final outburst is not on the horizon. Abandoning Mauss's cautious optimism that modern societies might recover the idea of the gift, Bataille has succeeded in justifying his preoccupation with the darker aspects of life, those obscure and obscene passages through which acts of excess may still be dimly witnessed and furtively performed as an impotent and reactionary protest against the boredom of unrestrained reason.

Bataille's private and inward revolt against the iron cage of rationalism apparently leaves little room for the social function of religion to shape and promote acts of abundance. Yet Bataille remains loyal throughout his works to the essentially mystical configuration of even the most erotic excesses. Mysticism is more than a metaphor. Loss is sacred, not frivolous. Transgression is buoyed by a sacramental power. Bataille is not advocating waste in the sense of unconstrained consumption, surely a message our gluttonous society does not need to hear. Spending sprees and cyclical binges are poor parodies of but perhaps typical contemporary substitutes for authentic acts of excess. True negation is propelled by a power of unarticulated absence that is capable of engulfing the self in a liberating free-fall into the abyss. To look deeper into this abyss is not to force an answer where Bataille only found problems but to seek further the source or the place where absence is experienced as if not redemptive then at least revelatory.

To return to the mystical texts of *Inner Experience* and *Guilty* in order to locate the power of absence is to find religious possibilities often overlooked by Bataille scholars and underdeveloped by Bataille himself. Theologians must decide how far they can follow Bataille, for whom the death of God does not signify a totally new, post-theistic, a-religious individual. Instead, the death of God is recapitulated in every free act, in every transgression. Excess not only depends on God's emptiness, but it is demanded by God's own self-overcoming. "I rely on God to deny himself, to loathe himself, to throw what he dares, what he is, into absence, into death," Bataille demands (*IE*, 131). Only a God who totally embraces the nothingness of death would be a God worthy of human acts of excess. In *Inner Experience* Bataille wonders, almost enviously, at the sacred horror of the *lema sabachthani*, where the summit of self-abandonment was reached in the confusion of a relentlessly total giving. The outline of the passion remains Bataille's model for the possibility of freedom within suffering.

The crucifixion is the passionate consummation of an irretrievable loss. This expenditure cannot be employed—invested—for any theological purpose. More than any other thinker, Bataille refuses to let his thought move from the crucifixion to the resurrection, from death to hope. Without the "how much more" or the "more than that" (Romans 8:34) of the resurrection, the crucifixion becomes a symbol of a giving that endorses suffering for its own sake.[31] Bataille mistakenly aligns his moving insight into the radically gratuitous nature of graced acts of giving with the expectation of certain frustration and ultimate defeat. Grace is not an excessive act that recognizes the other as the source of the self, funded by the eschatological promise of reciprocity and community. Instead, grace skirts the rim of the abyss in a dance that can only end in a spectacular but exhausted collapse. Grace rebounds on the giver, displaying an other whose distance denies satisfaction and a self who refuses to receive the guarantee that hope gives to giving.

Bataille is obsessed with loss, and he formulates his own passion in the shape of a strange prayer:

> Meaning of supplication. I express it thus, in the form of a prayer: O God our father, You who, in a night of despair, crucified Your son, who, in this night of butchery, as agony became *impossible*—to the point of distraction—became the *Impossible* Yourself and felt *impossibility* right to the point of horror—God of despair, give me that heart, Your heart, which fails, which exceeds all limits and tolerates no longer that you should be! (*IE*, 35)

In this only apparently sacrilegious prayer ("the night of butchery") surely we can see possibilities that Bataille himself did not fully pursue. The death of God is an event in which God so exceeds himself that God's experience of negation, of nothingness, leaves no room for himself. Language stretches but never can cover this ultimate absence. An extension with no promise of return is what Bataille seeks, and it is in the end God's own essence; the Christian God does not set up limitations but destroys God's self in order to make all things possible and new (Revelation 21:5).

God's death, so splendid and spectacular, can be so

terribly ultimate, but it can also invite us to embrace it, to follow God into the void, without hesitation or reflection. A disruptive loss of this magnitude seems unredeemable, and yet our capacity for imitation makes us wonder whether there is somewhere hope. In *Guilty* there is an astounding admission: "Endlessly beyond ourselves in absence, the desperate emptiness of pleasure would choke us—unless hope existed. In a way hope deceives, but how would it be possible to feel the attraction of the void if the appearance of the opposite wasn't also there?" (*G*, 155)[32] This hope cannot be known, but somehow, Bataille hints, it can be experienced as the power of absence itself. How, though, can excess open onto an absence that is not finally violent and self-destructive? At one point Bataille obliquely comments, "The crucifixion...is a wound by which believers communicate with God" (*G*, 31). Absence, loss, and sacrifice have a power to heal that belie the void across which they venture. God's death is long and painful, shuddering across history, beckoning—no, daring—us to follow into a senseless suffering that nevertheless promises what cannot dare be said.

Have I diluted Bataille's excess with a dose of theological obfuscation, forcing sense on the essentially irrational? To raise the issue of relevance—which is, after all, a question of use, work, productivity—near the perimeter of Bataille's discourse might seem brazenly inappropriate. Nevertheless, Bataille's language prompts certain questions about consequences and applications that even he did not disregard. Is excess in the end irrelevant, private, useless, a permanent detour away from the straight road of reason and civility? Does it serve a social function?[33] I will not deal completely with this question, of the relation between excess and purpose, until I turn to G. K. Chesterton in chapter 5. This middle, pivotal chapter shows that even great hyperboles, those that go too far in word and in deed, still must have a direction, still must be evaluated, still must hint at some sense. Excess alone is not enough. An indiscriminate expansion, an arbitrary enlargement, an impulsive amplification, does not constitute a good hyperbole. An exaggeration is a transformation of something toward something else. I discussed in chapter 2 Kierkegaard's conception of love as an infinite multiplier, subordinating the self to the other. I will follow in the next chapter the contours of an excess that violently moves toward a mystery of potentially redemptive significance. In the last chapter I will suggest ways in which religious persons can speak and enact an excess that makes sense by reaching out to others with acts that comfort and heal.

Here we have to wonder if Bataille does not go too far in his depiction of excess, risking an extravagance that deflates too quickly, a spontaneous spasm accomplishing nothing, a silent fluttering at the edges of existence. Is excess *in itself*, deliberate acts of waste, also *for itself*, or does it finally have an object, a goal, an economy? What is excess itself *for*? Although Bataille occasionally hints about a different way, his position is, on the whole, fairly consistent. We are fascinated by continuity but we always pull back, terrified of the suicidal impulse of excess. "We are incessantly trying to hoodwink ourselves, trying to get at continuity, which implies that the boundaries have been crossed, without actually crossing the boundaries of this discontinuous life" (*E*, 141). Something stops us from crossing a certain threshold, something as powerful as the hope without which any act of excess would be impossible. What is it? Not only can Bataille not name hope, but he also cannot name that which sends transgression back to the taboo, seeking protection, afraid of going too far— that which would put an end to Bataille's discourse, which is always struggling to say literally nothing, to fall apart in a useless explosion, to dissolve, to not make sense. To speak the end, the meaning or purpose of excess, would be a closure that Bataille's stammering, conceptually impoverished, cannot afford.

Bataille chooses against hope. His attack on meaning is tinged with a terrorist's desperation. The fact that

Bataille's excess is couched in violence and brutality
and tinged with giddiness and anxiety is not an incidental or merely biographical consideration. Bataille is a
playwright whose only character is a phenomenon that
repulses even as Bataille urgently tries to make it entice
and arouse. The many masks of excess—which, contrary to what Bataille sometimes claims, is never found
in any pure, undisguised form, but is always trapped in
an economy of representations as complicated as metaphysical systems and as spurious as mad gesticula-
tions—cannot hide its threatening strangeness and the
way it is unsatisfyingly doomed to fail to meet its own
promises. If hope were the last word we would not feel
so ambivalent about excess. In fact, what Bataille defi-
nitely has against God is that God guarantees that no
loss is final, that loss itself is not ultimately fundamental: God perturbs and haunts loss with the possibility of
hope, but God does this only by squandering God's self,
an expenditure that is so final, so agonizing, so spectacular that it resonates throughout Bataille's texts as their
hidden origin and their unsayable telos. Bataille plays
with but resists this path, a route he has only partly
opened and I have tried to further clear.

Indeed, the status of God's death is intentionally
confused in Bataille's discourse. To put my own diver-
gence from Bataille simply: Is God's death something
real in itself that nonetheless gives birth to hope *or* is it
merely a symbol that prefigures our own death, which
each of us must face alone as we squander ourselves
into the void? For Bataille, excess is not empowered by
a sense of adventure and discovery, by possibilities and
opportunities, by healing as well as pain due to the
boundless and infinite suffering of God. Excess does
not open the self to an other who understands; it does
not give to an other who needs and demands. In his
frantic attempt to sever sacrifice from an economy of
expenditure and return, to liberate negation from the
omnipresent encroachment of the recuperative capacity of rationality, to disconnect authenticity from

morality, Bataille can only imagine excess as a force that directs life always elsewhere. This great exponent of excess inscribes extravagance within an economy that permits escape only at the expense of life itself. Calculative rationality and an aesthetic of moderation are granted such enormous power that their violation entails a regressive return to the undifferentiated helplessness of the infantile state. Excess does not reach out to find the other in ecstatic acts of mutual recognition and intersubjective enjoyment. The disorienting effect of excess makes it essentially aimless. Excess cannot be followed to the end by Bataille because for him it actually leads nowhere; it cannot be written because it ends in nothing. It cannot be enclosed because it is the closure. Indeed, in the very ends of Bataille's many excesses a content does appear, hyperbole displays a referent, sacrifice a goal, and its name is death. This unspoken finality of Bataille's various discourses still leaves us, though, as an unintended remainder, the question of whose death and why.

Chapter
Four

Life Over the Edges:
Flannery O'Connor's Dis-Grace-Full Extremity

The road of excess leads to the palace of wisdom.
William Blake, Proverbs of Hell

"Out, hyperbolical fiend!"
Shakespeare, Twelfth Night

To read Flannery O'Connor—one of this country's most discussed authors—in a nontheological manner by now must surely be regarded as an insolent act of blindness that only she could fully appreciate. Nevertheless, the relation of her disorienting stories to her orthodox Roman Catholic religious views has caused a polarization in the secondary literature that is apparently impossible to reconcile. Many studies bracket O'Connor's apologetical intentions without completely ignoring her religious perspective by arguing that she inadvertently speaks for the devil: she creates stories full of undefeated demons and thus advocates a secret nihilism, without any redeeming or resolving conclusions.[1] Some theological analyses, in direct opposition to this position, unfortunately credit her own reflections with the final word on this hermeneutical debate. They tend to treat her fiction as a cloak or guise for religious ideas, moving prematurely from the rhetorical to the spiritual.[2] The common argument is that for our

postmodern era her work constitutes the supreme
example of a theological *via negativa*, portraying a distorted, ugly, and yet comical world in which a very real
but usually unrecognized imposition of grace combats
an insidious force of evil in order to drive characters
beyond themselves—and against their own poorly
understood desires—to God.

Between these two opposite and extreme sets of
readings lies O'Connor's own ambiguously excessive and
painfully contorted fictive terrain.[3] All the secondary literature agrees that she is a master of excess, a prophet of
extremity, but her interpreters bitterly contest for what
purposes she deploys such distortion and deception.
Perhaps the problem centers on hyperbole itself. Indeed,
even though hyperbole is often mentioned in O'Connor
studies,[4] it is rarely used in any extensive or methodical
way to illuminate her literary vision. I want to wager that
the pursuit of hyperbole in her stories will go a long way
toward locating, even if not resolving, the religious significance of her fiction. Her corpus is dramatic proof of
the power and subtlety of exaggeration, but it is also evidence of the ambiguity and risks of this trope. Unlike
Kierkegaard, she does not hyperbolically extol the power
of love, nor does she, following Bataille, subordinate all
concerns to pure excess itself. She utilizes hyperbole
without restricting or containing it to get at truths that
uniquely belong to that trope's domain. From a carefully
controlled point of view (she always uses the omniscient
narrative voice), she renders her ordinary, even earthy
characters in wickedly distorted forms, pushing them
further than any reader might think possible, and thus
produces a powerful meditation on the ability of the
artist to harness—constrain, distill, and considerately
craft—hyperbole in order to explode all limitations and
expectations.

Her calibrated tone, frequently understated and
deceptively modest, frames a reckless and effusive
power that drives her characters over the brink; ruthlessly and analytically, her objective voice explores not

life on the edges of the ordinary, but life cast over the edge—the moment in which characters, *sub specie aeternitatis*, are pushed beyond themselves, dissolved by their own limitations, suspended in a self-knowledge that is neither welcomed nor understood. Her stories explore the power of hyperbole without moralizing or theorizing—or theologizing—on its capacity to restore, fit, and make sense. Even her own reflections, though admittedly they sometimes contextualize hyperbole in dogmatic theological explanations, actually show that she was more aware of the intricate contours of this configuration than some of her critics allow. More than any other writer, she follows hyperbole across the borders of conventional emplotment and characterization toward realities unknown, creating a literary world that can be empathetically entered only at the risk of a disorienting and potentially inconclusive journey.

Her stories, at once both surreal and primitive, frequently have been called grotesque, probably due to her attraction to freaks and fanatics, one-legged and morally maimed intellectuals, grandiose prophets, and spiritually mangled mystics. The term "grotesque," for all of its helpful vividness, is closely related to hyperbole and equally difficult to define. It records the ability of something contrary to mundane reality—the taboo, ugly, or monstrous—to arrest our attention while leaving our understanding, groping after the intrusive and forcible other, unsatisfied. As Geoffrey Galt Harpham explains, "As an adjective it has no descriptive value; its sole function is to represent a condition of overcrowding or contradiction in the place where the modifier should be."[5] The grotesque figure is simultaneously fascinating and repulsive, even terrifying. Harpham calls such figures hybrids, something stuck between two realities without a mediating or synthesizing principle.

Although Harpham does not use hyperbole to illuminate the grotesque, that relationship is important. In opposition to metaphor, which confirms our faith in the interconnectedness of reality and the strength of our own imaginations by drawing together disparate realms into a single organic image, the grotesque threatens to show us that what really is is more than we could ever possibly understand. Simultaneously invoking and discrediting representation, it does not reconcile two opposites but begins with the ordinary and, not gently but abruptly, makes it not just extraordinary but otherworldly, all the while insisting on its own verity. It drives reality beyond itself toward contradiction without becoming impossible or mythological.[6] Denying the vision that sees total otherness as something either spatially set apart from the here and now or imaginatively identical to what we already know, it portrays a dimension to existence that makes an ontological claim that defies the logic of both the otherworldly and the everyday.

In our post-Holocaust world it is natural to suspect that the sublime can be found, if at all, only in the grotesque. Indeed, in a world of moral and physical chaos, it can be doubted whether we can so readily recognize and name the grotesque, let alone the sublime, anymore. As O'Connor perceptively notes, "The problem may well become one of finding something that is *not* grotesque and of deciding what standards we would use in looking."[7] What is troubling is that, like hyperbole, the grotesque appears to be a relative gesture, dependent on some recognition of a prior order, while at the same time it shows how easily order, seen from a certain angle, slides into chaos. While O'Connor's Roman Catholic faith certainly enabled her to see the grotesque with a sharp eye, she did not presuppose a common consent to order that the grotesque then disrupts. "The world is almost rotten," the heartless Mr. Shiftlet (under)states in "The Life You Save May Be Your Own." The "almost" is a nagging qualification, leaving open the possibility that evil is not the last word, but frustrating any elaboration. Rejecting Manichaean dualism, the compartmentalization of evil and good, O'Connor always allows the grotesque to erupt from within the ordinary, extending, like a good hyperbole, the accepted to the point where it becomes, perhaps, unacceptable.

As opposed to the gothic, where terror is used to fix and sustain a special atmosphere, the grotesque raises what are essentially metaphysical problems.[8] By exaggerating deformity and horror, they become something other than what they are: the unbearable is made fascinating. The demonic is fully revealed because there is the faint promise that it can be thereby subdued, and the ugly is empowered by being imbued with a sense of mystery and menace. The sudden and stark violence of many of O'Connor's stories is both what it really is, that is, evil, and a figure for something other—spiritual warfare. Her apocalyptic endings—recall the fusion of baptism and suicide in "The River"—are not mere riddles but explosions in which the reader too is a potential victim. Even her celebrated sense of place and use of idiom is deceptive; the local is heightened in order to drive it toward the universal.

By means of hyperbole, the term grotesque is related to another concept helpful for O'Connor studies, melodrama. Some scholars have argued that melodrama is a noun, not an adjective, denoting a specific genre of literature,[9] while more often melodrama is used, pejoratively or not, to represent the theatrical impulse itself, even when it is embedded in literature. The term conjures lurid and grotesque events, disguised identities, abductions and slow working poisons, and a very real, even if hidden, presence of evil. Peter Brooks suggests that melodramatic stories can be described according to

the extravagance of certain representations, and the intensity of moral claim impinging on their characters' consciousness. Within an apparent context of "realism" and the ordinary, they seemed in fact to be staging a heightened and hyperbolic

drama, making reference to pure and polar concepts of darkness and light, salvation and damnation.[10]

In totally expressive gestures and actions, melodrama
concentrates a moral vision of the polarized nature of
good and evil. The smallest details can signal an escalation of meaning that is overwhelming in significance
and power. "Nothing is understood, all is overstated."[11]
In melodrama, due to hyperbole, everything is meaningful.

The risk of melodrama, as with hyperbole, is that it
will appear to be self-indulgent and histrionic, and like
hyperbole, the term covers a broad range of expressions, not all of which do justice to its complexity and
importance. Perhaps in its simplest form, melodrama
can mean quite precisely nothing more than just excess
itself. Indeed, Brooks describes melodrama as a victory
over repression and thus a triumph of desire: "The
melodramatic utterance breaks through everything that
constitutes the 'reality principle,' all its censorships,
accommodations, tonings-down."[12] Melodrama is scan-
dalous and embarrassing and, perhaps worst of all from
the viewpoint of the academy, like hyperbole it is
unscholarly. It seemingly rejects ambiguity and subtlety in a complete externalization of emotion and fore-
grounding of depth.[13] It is a discourse liberated from all
pragmatic constraint.

Brooks also, however, attempts to redeem melodrama from its low status in the arts by finding in it a
socially relevant function. Melodrama, he argues, tries
to recover a sense of morality in a postreligious culture.

The heightening and hyperbole, the polarized conflict, the menace and suspense of the representations may be made necessary by the effort to
perceive and image the spiritual in a world voided
of its traditional Sacred, where the body of the ethical has become a sort of *deus absconditus* which

must be sought for, postulated, brought into man's existence through the play of the spiritualist imagination. (11)

In a world in which the moral has become disconnected from the spiritual, the excesses of melodrama are a necessary corrective to a nihilistic climate. A moral vision without any cultural support or theological justification will be, Brooks seems to be saying, necessarily melodramatic. Melodrama represents, then, the only way in which we can speak morally in an age when we cannot take morality seriously anymore.

O'Connor was always acutely aware that she was considered a member of the Southern School, which "conjures up an image of Gothic monstrosities and the idea of a preoccupation with everything deformed and grotesque" (*MM*, 28). She also, however, always tries to let her moral sense coincide with her dramatic vision, to make moral judgment "a part of the very act of seeing" (*MM*, 31). Her use of hyperbole and its allies, melodrama and the grotesque, is never incidental or ostentatious. In a crucial statement on her style, she explains her reliance on distortion:

> The novelist with Christian concerns will find in modern life distortions which are repugnant to him, and his problem will be to make these appear as distortions to an audience which is used to seeing them as natural; and he may well be forced to take ever more violent means to get his vision across to this hostile audience. When you can assume that your audience holds the same beliefs you do, you can relax a little and use more normal means of talking to it; when you have to assume that it does not, then you have to make your vision apparent by shock—to the hard of hearing you draw large and startling figures. (*MM*, 33–34)

The Christian artist, a member of a minority facing a hostile world, cannot afford to assure, celebrate, or affirm;[14] instead, unable to rely on a common sense of clarity, O'Connor's distortions are situated along the lines of both an attack and an investigation into the truth. The result is that they reveal their truest literary vision when appearances are not what they seem.

Unlike Brooks's analysis of melodrama as unsublimated morality, O'Connor's hyperboles are an expression of alienation as well as an aggressive affront to modernity. Hyperbole is not a substitute or compensation; it does not replace or correct something else. O'Connor uses distortion not to depict a pure and post-decadent morality but to display a superfluous spirituality which cannot see itself clearly. Her characters are hybrid not in the sense that they are in between this world and the next but in the way in which their self-understandings are but a mockery of who they really are. When the spiritual has become so totally other that it is no longer relevant to the modern world—the orthodox predilection for order and balance, the sense that the spiritual is spatially fixed in different but related levels, is irretrievably gone—hyperbole shows that within this world, seen clearly through the lens of distortion, the "other" is already here. For the Christian to speak to the secular world, then, hyperbole is a necessary tool, but it is more than that; where reality itself fails, hyperbole reveals.

Hyperbole constitutes its own version of reality, every bit as true as more literal descriptions. Indeed, O'Connor always insists on being a realist.[15] The Prophet is a realist of distances, she was fond of saying: nearby things, seen intently, extend meaningfully beyond the obvious, while things far away, the mysteries of other worlds, are deeply embedded in the manners of the everyday. She has a vertical, not a horizontal range; with a limited set of scenes and topics, the unlimited forces its way through restrictions that serve to release the unknown.[16] In the Christ-haunted South, which has traditionally opposed Enlightenment, optimistic views of human nature, this style is especially appropriate; a mirror could never catch all that goes without saying but nevertheless must be said. In the grotesque, she explains,

> We find that connections which we would expect in the customary kind of realism have been ignored, that there are strange slips and gaps which anyone trying to describe manners and customs would certainly not have left. Yet the characters have an inner coherence, if not always a coherence to their social framework. Their fictional qualities lean away from typical social patterns, toward mystery and the unexpected. (*MM*, 40)

The writer who believes in mystery will push the limits of the story outward, where meaning takes off as description falls short, but also where events are still concrete and characters are, if not familiar, at least persuasive. Hyperbole does not say everything, but it says just enough to say too much, and thus says the most important things.

O'Connor's prose says those important things with a raging and cutting vigor that demonstrates one of the fundamental facts of hyperbole: to counter prevailing attitudes in excessive form is an act of violence. Her most violent story, "A Good Man is Hard to Find," couples a Misfit who revels in his rejection of Jesus but sullenly admits, "It's no real pleasure in life," with a self-satisfied grandmother whose only pleasure is pride. When she reaches out to touch him (after her family has been massacred), recognizing him as one of her own, he shoots her, saying, "She would of been a good woman if it had been somebody there to shoot her every minute of her life." The reader is left agreeing with the Misfit that "Jesus thrown everything off balance," but there is no hint of any solution except for the comical thought that goodness comes—too late—at the point of a gun. In talking about the title of her second novel, *The Violent Bear It Away*, O'Connor justifies herself: "The kingdom of heaven has to be taken by violence or not at all. You have to push as hard as the age that pushes against you" (*HB*, 229). O'Connor's fiction literalizes the metaphor of spiritual warfare.

The most immediate victims of O'Connor's violence are her very own characters, and she is often criticized for her apparent lack of sympathy for her own creations. Her persistent reliance on violence to affect a narrative turn of events—and to shove her readers past where her characters end—is troubling in its seemingly reckless disregard for her characters' dignity and integrity. The drastic choice in *The Violent Bear It Away* between fundamentalism (Old Tarwater) and modernism (Rayber) is forced on young Tarwater as a relentless either/or in which he finds his vocation, his calling, only after a confrontation with evil that takes the form of a literal rape. Her comment about the optimistic liberalism of Sheppard, the father in "The Lame Shall Enter First" is equally cold and brutally direct: "He had stuffed his own emptiness with good works like a glutton." Indeed, the father's attempt to help (to shepherd) the clubfooted Rufus, who literally eats a page from the Bible in order to reject the father's condescending atheism, leads him to neglect his son, Norton, who searches for his dead mother in the stars. Sheppard meets his due punishment when he finds Norton hanging in the attic, "in the jungle of the shadows, just below the beam from which he had launched his flight into space." Norton, fed with images of heaven and hell by the unrepentant and yet dogmatic Rufus, can lift his imagination only as high as outer space, literally seeing his mother as a star-bright speck of love shining through to the darkness of his cold home, and reaches out to her, in fulfillment of the story's title, in the only way that he knows how.

In her defense, O'Connor did argue that the grotesque is not a compassionate trope; it teaches hard lessons. "The intellectual and moral judgments implicit in it," O'Connor warns, "will have ascendancy over feeling" (*MM*, 43). She often suggests, in fact, that the reason she was so good at recognizing freaks was that she had some definite, that is, theological conception of the whole person.[17] Nevertheless, her deformed characters—blinded by an excess of will, intruding upon the good, seeking to use it, to claim it, only to find themselves out of safe territory and dangerously overextended—do not immediately imply more wholesome doubles. "It's not necessary to point out," she admits, "that the look of this fiction is going to be wild, that it is almost of necessity going to be violent and comic, because of the discrepancies that it seeks to combine" (*MM*, 43). Unlike metaphor, hyperbole does not hint at cohesion and unity; it does not combine but breaks apart, leaving fragmented any synthesis that might heal broken spirits and mutilated intellects.

In spite of this violence, however, O'Connor always expresses a blessed rage that does not seek either to destroy or restore but to extend and reveal. In her own words, she sought to "distort without destroying" (*MM*, 50)[18] in order to teach her readers to see clearly. The novelist's journey, she writes, "will be a descent through the darkness of the familiar into a world where, like the blind man cured in the gospels, he sees men as if they were trees, but walking" (*MM*, 50). Some distortions are so clear that they are like seeing something for the very first time.[19] Out of the accumulation of warped detail arises a sudden rush of mystery that the perspective of the ordinary refuses to recognize. It is no surprise that this mystery, which she always names as grace, will strike many readers as a violent assault. "Our age does not have a very sharp eye for the almost imperceptible intrusions of grace, it no longer has much feeling for the nature of the violences which precede and follow them" (*MM*, 112). To teach (blind) readers to see is a painful operation.

O'Connor's talk of violence not only points to a central feature of hyperbole but also displays a crucial ambiguity. In her reflective afterthoughts on her own work, she sometimes tends to treat hyperbole as a pedagogical tool, useful for theological purposes, controlled by a stern, Godlike narrative voice, with the aim of judging and redeeming her sinbound characters. When the mean-spirited Mr. Shiftlet, in his ill-gained car surrounded by menacing clouds and "fantastic rain-drops, like tin-can tops," races "the galloping shower into Mobile," we can feel the anger of the narrator in the storm that is chasing him into the city. Hyperbole's violence, from this perspective, is ultimately educative, a kind of shock therapy. "In my own stories I have found that violence is strangely capable of returning my characters to reality and preparing them to accept their moment of grace" (MM, 112). The movement outward is carried aloft by the guarantee of a compensatory return.

Implied here is a rather romantic notion of grace: it comes but once in each individual's life, at that moment when it is least expected but when the most consequences are at stake.[20] The compressed description of Mrs. May's absurd death in "Greenleaf," for example, ignites this fusion of violence, grace and resolution. "She stared at the violent black streak bounding toward her as if she had no sense of distance, as if she could not decide at once what his intention was, and the bull had buried his head in her lap, like a wild tormented lover, before her expression changed." The reader follows this long sentence, which delays the bull's bounding streak by Mrs. May's own incomprehension, from Mrs. May's hesitation, as if something is demanded of her, to the grotesque image of the lover/bull and finally stumbles upon the defusingly calm "her expression changed," melodramatically denying death the last word.

Grace thus serves as the ultimate turning point in a narrative as well as the perfect (non)ending: closure is not articulated within the framework of the narrative but is pointed to, hinted at, approached like a corner that cannot yet be turned. The danger is that grace is subordinated to the demands of emplotment; it is the ending that never quite can be written, but if it were it would point to a new and wonderful beginning. At one point, she puts forward this position as a general hermeneutical principle: "There is a moment in every great story in which the presence of grace can be felt as it waits to be accepted or rejected, even though the reader may not recognize this moment" (*MM*, 118). Grace, in the form of turning points, is what makes all good stories effective.

Such graced hyperbole, however, would hardly qualify as violent; it would be like the surgical cut that wounds only to heal.[21] Indeed, O'Connor's characters are frequently nothing less than markers that portend an essential tension, instabilities on the verge of eternity, unknowing victims of a cosmic clash between good and evil, and if hyperbole pushes them off the edge, it is only, perhaps, for their own good. The moralistic side of O'Connor is most vividly displayed in "An Enduring Chill," where the intensification of Asbury's illness is editorialized in the last line of the story: "But the Holy Ghost emblazoned in ice instead of fire, continued, implacable, to descend." Asbury's chill becomes terribly purifying, but O'Connor's verdict too easily concludes this melodrama about a young man whose pride could be deflated only by the comedy of his various self-misunderstandings.

Her stories work better when the uncanny erupts from, rather than being imposed upon, the narrative. This is the case in "Good Country People" where Joy, a Ph.D. in philosophy who has defiantly changed her name to Hulga, is blandly described as "a large blonde girl who had an artificial leg" and makes her mother, Mrs. Hopewell, think of "the broad blank hull of a battleship." Her wooden leg grows as a symbol continuously throughout the story until it is stolen by a cynical Bible salesman, at which point its absence becomes painfully revelatory. A similar subtlety occurs in "Everything that Rises Must Converge." Julian, stripped of his pride and confronted with a love that he cannot articulate, is on the edge not of judgment or redemption but a kind of purgatory, fading into a tide of darkness "postponing from moment to moment his entry into the world of guilt and sorrow." Grace allows the story not to end but to demand, not to conclude but to imply; it creates the space that signifies what the end always is, a very present absence.[22]

Such gradual or sudden swells of meaning are difficult to interpret, and O'Connor was often tempted to defuse her hyperboles by reducing them not only to a theology of grace but also, even more abstractly, to a philosophy of extremity. "It is the extreme situation," she writes, "that best reveals what we are essentially" (*MM*, 113). Frederick Asals has followed this line of reflection, arguing that O'Connor's work constitutes a systematic fictive treatment of extremity as an end in itself. By using an ironic detachment of the narrative voice and, frequently, the motif of the threatening double, O'Connor's antipodal perspectives push her characters beyond themselves into a region that even her own prose, resisting any simple closure, hesitates to follow. "Rather than merging, blending, informing one another," Asals explains, "[O'Connor's polarities] are sustained in a set of vibrant tensions that seem to open ever wider, to strain furiously toward a breaking point."[23] This all or nothing style suggests a philosophical point. "The middle is always mediocre in O'Connor, a condition ultimately of illusion, for in the world she dramatizes only extremes have genuine existence."[24] In this off balance world there is no via media, no mediation of the tensions that usurp the center and send characters to the edges, running for cover.

Asals's analysis is insightful, but he often writes as if extremity were some thing—in the plot or the characters—that can be isolated in O'Connor's works, and that her stories are, in the end, about extremity itself. I want to suggest that extremity of situation and characterization—which is often only indirectly, ironically depicted by O'Connor—is not portrayed as a position in its own right but as a transition that cannot be fully followed by

artistic form. Whether hyperbole is abruptly forced
upon or deceptively insinuated into her stories, like
grace its disruptive power cannot be easily understood
or predicted. O'Connor does not romantically glorify life
at the extremes; she does not afford the reader the luxury of pausing in nihilistic abandonment to test life at
its most intense. She is a hillbilly Thomist, she occasionally said, not a hillbilly nihilist. Better yet, she is an
explorer of extremity, but not in order to find in it some
self-sufficient station of life on the margins. Instead, she
tries to show that when life oversteps itself, dis-grace-
fully reaching beyond its limits—as it is bound to do—it
goes over the edges; at the moment of extremity there
are no guarantees, and terror is just as possible as grace.

To insure this urgent sense of mystery, the hidden
agency of God, and the suddenness of grace, O'Connor's
most typical ploy is to sharpen her perception of evil,
heightening and intensifying it to the point where it
becomes personified not as a vague spirit but as the
demonic. "My subject in fiction is the action of grace in
territory held largely by the devil" (*MM*, 118).[25] In a
world that refuses to recognize itself as drenched in
evil, grace must be presented as indirect and aggressive, using strategies of deception and entrapment to
undermine casual assumptions and vague intentions.
Mystery, which is an embarrassment to the modern
mind, is insinuated only through its opposite, disclosed
only through the eruption of evil. Grace is not pious,
sentimental, or nostalgic; it does not represent some
pure state, illusory wish, or naive emotion. In O'Connor's stories grace is hardened into an objective even if
unseen force, something you do not experience, desire,
or feel but something that is nonetheless powerful,
active, and concrete. "The action of grace changes a
character. Grace can't be experienced in itself" (*HB*,
275). Grace is depicted only as a cruel contradiction of
evil, while evil itself, too often domesticated, rationalized and naturalized by optimistic and progressive presuppositions, is exaggerated to do justice to grace.

Grace is thus an unbearably compressed pressure at the heart of being, ever ready to explode in judgment and, the reader is often left to hope, redemption.

Indirect routes are always precarious. By seeking the positive only through the negative, O'Connor realizes that she risks sending ambiguous messages— voices mired in static—through her works. If she goes too far in intensifying the violence of hyperbole and giving authentic utterance to the demonic, her prose might stray from her orthodox theological goals. Can such hyperbole, once unleashed, really be so easily tamed? The artist, O'Connor realizes, "may find in the end that instead of reflecting the image at the heart of things, he has only reflected our broken condition, and through it, the face of the devil we are possessed by" (*MM*, 168). Poorly written novels can never be really edifying, O'Connor argues, and conversely, really good novels risk giving up edification. The dire descent of the novelist does not guarantee an equivalent and compensating ascent.

Following hyperbole is a blinding journey; its violent energy cannot be easily diverted into productive channels. O'Connor, for all of her theological beliefs, understood that the creation of fiction is very different from the propagation of faith. She usually does not try to impose an agenda on her own stories, no matter how strict and unwavering were her beliefs. By trying to treat grace surreptitiously, she risks letting it slip completely away. "Of course you are only enabled to see what is black by having light to see it by," she acknowledges, " [but] the light you see by may be altogether outside of the work itself" (*HB*, 173). Her stories capture the piercing illumination but not the glowing source of grace, shadows instead of light, and thus she knew that her work could be interpreted in many different ways: "Much of my fiction takes its character from a reasonable use of the unreasonable, though the reasonableness of my use of it may not always be apparent" (*MM*, 109). Her own aims could become submerged in the diabolical plots and demonic characters in which she reveled.[26]

Her stories do not recount her own spiritual inner life but constitute a detour through many religious manifestations that must have been ultimately alien to her own sensibilities.[27] "The Catholic novelist in the South is forced to follow the spirit into strange places and to recognize it in many forms not totally congenial to him" (*MM*, 206). Her perverse kinship with backwoods fundamentalists—she always writes about the most extreme forms of Protestantism—allowed her to neglect the more civil and polite aspects of religion in order to delve directly into spirituality in its most strenuous and grotesque forms.[28] In spite of trying to move these spiritual misfits—displaced persons, as the title of one of her stories puts it—toward the wholeness of the church, she risks damning them without redemption. "It is very possible that what is vision and truth to the writer is temptation and sin to the reader" (*MM*, 187). The reader cannot be expected to follow hyperbole precisely to where O'Connor wanted it to go. Even O'Connor herself was not always certain about the path her fiction had taken. As her own first reader, then, O'Connor is an invaluable lesson about the hopes, and the risks, of hyperbole taken to the limits.

To ignore such a crucial first reader would be just as foolish as to substitute first readings for seconds, thirds, and more. Yet, no one can approach an O'Connor story without keeping in mind her own thoughts and reflections. When and how, if at all, do the distortions start to make sense, and do they make the sense that O'Connor intended? On a first reading, and even after many subsequent interpretations, the reader is inevitably drawn to O'Connor's (non)endings, eerie and uncanny, although the connections and discontinuities between the endings and the rest of the stories usually give them their special impact. Do these equivocal endings (often masquerading as impossible beginnings) stretch the characters out of their usual shape and

thereby provide some contact point between the natural and the divine, or do they explode all expectations
and frustrate all explanations by perverting the ordinary and making it absurd? Do they promise, however
obliquely, salvation, or do they deliver damnation? Do
they hint at something other, or display an utterly hor-
rifying nothingness? Do they offer grace, or dis-grace,
or is everything both suspended and held in check by
an inconspicuous and yet mocking narrative voice?

An early story originally published in 1949, "A
Stroke of Good Fortune," demonstrates the significance
of these possibly futile questions. The story centers
around Ruby, who is concerned above all to be better
than other people and who therefore spends much of
her time comparing herself to others. A palm reader has
predicted that a long illness will bring her a stroke of
good fortune, and the reader finds her, in fact, alone
and breathless on the flight of stairs leading to her
apartment. As she climbs and stops to catch her breath,
she sees Hartley, the son of a neighbor, nicknamed Little Mister Good Fortune, and talks to a friend, who surprises her with the vehemently denied suspicion that
she is pregnant. During her last assault on the stairs
she falters, Hartley crashes into her, and she says,
clutching the banister, "Good Fortune, Baby." The
comma says more than the words themselves. Is she
speaking to Hartley, or connecting the palmist's predic-
tion with her own fears about her possible pregnancy?

The three last lines of the story take increasingly
dramatic leaps. "Then she recognized the feeling again,
a little roll. It was as if it were not in her stomach. It was
as if it were out nowhere in nothing, out nowhere, rest-
ing and waiting, with plenty of time." The lines, at first
short and tight, stretch the thought of pregnancy
toward a deeper, more oblique expectation. The little
roll quickly becomes identified first with something
external and objective and then with a dynamic and
threatening absence. The "as if" construction, common
in O'Connor's stories, does not create some metaphori-

cal image but prompts the imagination toward other, unspoken connections. Ruby's world is going to change, we suspect, but our own knowledge is no more secure than hers. The last line has a sudden urgency in which the images of birth and death, of Hartley and her own possible baby, are not drawn together but pushed forward, leaving a space that only our imaginations can fill. Perhaps that is the point. Only with this sudden escalation, made possible by Ruby's own limitations, can we begin to see Ruby in a new light, but we know the light only by its shadows.

This story sets a pattern that the others will deepen and broaden, encroaching more violently upon both the sacred and the profane. In "A Temple of the Holy Ghost," a twelve-year-old girl, eaten up with pride and sarcasm, hears about a hermaphrodite who claims to be a temple of the Holy Ghost. She is brought to an epiphany of apocalyptic proportions:

> Her mother let the conversation drop and the child's round face was lost in thought. She turned it toward the window and looked out over a stretch of pasture land that rose and fell with a gathering greenness until it touched the dark woods. The sun was a huge red ball like an elevated Host drenched in blood and when it sank out of sight, it left a line in the sky like a red clay road hanging over the trees.

The verbs are mild and passive: let drop and was lost, turned and looked, rose and fell and touched. Each sentence, however, gathers itself to leap further than the previous one could ever lead the reader to expect. The lost round face turns in the second sentence to see a gathering greenness touching a dark woods. These languid images are transposed by the whole instant of a revelation expressed in the overstuffed final statement. The red ball sun (shaped like the round face) drenched in eucharistic blood and leaving a line like red clay (the red starkly complements the gathering greenness) sinks (like the conversation drops and the pasture falls) and hangs over the trees (suspended like the young girl's thoughts). In all of this movement there is a stillness that portends something sacramental that the language can no longer follow.

These impossible endings reach their apotheosis in "Revelation," a story that cannot be summarized. Mrs. Turpin sits proudly in a doctor's waiting room, a ghoulish scene where the vain, the ugly, the ignorant, and the all but dead have gathered hoping to be healed but acting "as if they would sit there until Doomsday if nobody called them and told them to get up." Doomsday, in fact, occurs. Mrs. Turpin, whom the most generous reader will surely regard as unpleasant, full of condescension and self-righteousness, takes the greatest pleasure in being neither black nor "poor white trash." Her inane conversation is abruptly halted by the unhappy college student, Mary Grace, who throws a book at her just as Mrs. Turpin decides that everything is just the way it should be. "Go back to hell where you came from, you old wart hog," Mary Grace whispers, and the reader surely laughs and cheers.

Nevertheless, Mrs. Turpin, unsettled and standing outside a pig parlor, is granted a remarkable vision, so odd that it seems plausible, in which "a vast horde of souls were rumbling toward heaven." At the end of the migration were people just like herself, proud, secure, and self-satisfied white people, marching with dignity and respect. "Yet she could see by their shocked and altered faces that even their virtues were being burned away." The narrative voice does not try to idealize the vision; Mrs. Turpin is still the same person, and sees her vices as virtues. The people like herself "alone were on key," yet they were shocked, and for once O'Connor does not let her incredible ending stop short, hinting at everything and saying nothing. With unexpected modesty and humility, she lets Mrs. Turpin step down from the pigs, accompanied by a chorus of crickets, and make her way back to the house, still hearing the voices of those souls shouting hallelujah. For once—and this story is one of the last O'Connor wrote before the disease lupus finally silenced her—a character, and the reader with her, is allowed to turn a gentle back on all the hyperbole, to think about it as she turns away, neither slain nor saved, but haunted. In this ending, hyperbole is understated, undeveloped, unwritten, and unsaid; like grace itself it is the something more that, nevertheless, is best left to silence, because one can never say enough to say it.

Theologically speaking, in O'Connor's stories the supernatural becomes the hyperbolic; only through saying too much can that be said which cannot be said at all, but of course the too much can never be fully articulated. "A God you understand would be less than yourself" (*HB*, 354). The supernatural here is not spatially represented, a level of existence set apart. Instead, access to the supernatural is granted only by distortion, which is the accurate depiction of life at the limits. At their limits, O'Connor's characters can discover that they do not have a center, have nothing to hold. In opposition to Kant's program of limiting knowledge in order to make room for faith, leaving God unknown but nevertheless real, O'Connor approaches God through the known by pushing it past what it is thought to be. The supernatural becomes a remnant, a mute survival of a violent collision, an unknown barrier that both obstructs and explodes. Hyperbole pushes characters so far that, before the reader knows it, the reader follows them over the edge, either into the void or the bosom of God. Sometimes, in fact, the reader is left hanging, but whether by the neck or the fingertips is uncertain. The mystery is always behind our backs; we can never turn around fast enough to grasp it, but we can learn to sense its presence, even in its disruptive absence. These stories are rearguard actions, and the climaxes signal an attack from a hidden enemy, unnamed but nevertheless powerfully effective.

This theological reading, however subtle, is admittedly troubling. Is her fiction, in the end, apologetical in the most traditional sense of that term, illustrating the ironclad law of sin and redemption, tracing the plummeting path of the soul stubbornly turned against God? "Some kind of loss is usually necessary to turn the mind toward faith," she states. "If you're satisfied with what you've got, you're hardly going to look for anything better" (*HB*, 159).[29] Is her point of view not only Godlike, but representative of the very God, objective, observant, but in the end remorseless and removed, leaving characters free to follow their own deluded desires and blinded ideas into damnation? The distanciation of the narrative voice is unnerving. Does she offer her characters utter freedom only to have them succumb to the inevitable effects of sin? In other words, is her fiction really theology? Does she provide a fictive transformation of theology that in the end restores grace to its proper sphere, her eucharistic stories effecting the conversion that the church too performs?[30]

There is a moral question about apologetics today, whether in a world of such excessive suffering the theologian should make use of the failure of modernity to show the need for something other. As Carol Shloss perceptively explains, "For a statement of faith is easier for an agnostic reader to accept than O'Connor's usual tendency toward oblique insult, which ensues from the intimation that her fictional world is fraught with portentous meanings that we could see if only we were not such monstrous readers, and too limited to understand."[31] What is insinuated is that straight-forward confessional theology is more honest—and pays its audience more respect—than the incorrigibly deceptive indirection, with its implicit division of the audience into insiders and outsiders, of a theology hidden in distorted literary guise. Dietrich Bonhoeffer was the most notable proponent of this argument: the theologian should not attack the adulthood of the world, trying, from resentment, to make room for religion by criticizing the very positive gains of secularity.[32] In sum, if you seek to reassert the sacred into the willfully profane, you should be open and honest about what you are trying to do.

The problem with Schloss's criticism is that hyperbole is not such a direct assault; once launched, it cannot be so easily directed, and this ambiguity gives O'Connor's stories more than, but not less than, apologetical significance. For O'Connor, the religious quest, coupled with grotesque perception and melodramatic gestures, strains after a transcendence that is revealed at best only negatively as an abrupt and shattering return to reality. The spiritual is necessarily distorted in our age; its grotesque appearance to modern sensibilities is not merely a rhetorical move for O'Connor. It is an ontological statement about the world as we now see it. Indeed, O'Connor does not pretend to lift up reality to some higher level; instead she wants to disclose the really real, in spite of itself. For a reality constantly at odds with itself, hyperbole seems to be the only road that takes us home by taking us far, far away. Hyperbole does not display the spiritual as another level of reality, something that has been forgotten or misunderstood. It does not widen our perspectives to include something peripheral or hidden. It begins with what we all already know and drives our knowledge deeper and deeper, disorienting us by turning the real against itself, until, calling on our courage, the certainty stops making sense.[33] Hyperbole enlarges and expands, but only with a violence (as Bataille understood) that cannot guarantee its outcome. Everything that rises must converge: yes, indeed, but the convergence is only momentarily and partially glimpsed, and at what terrific cost.

Chapter Five

Excess (Un)Bound:
G. K. Chesterton and
the Question of Orthodoxy

The true way we may go unto His Throne, and can never
Exceed, nor be too High. All Hyperboles are but little
Pigmies, and Diminutiv Expressions, in Comparison of
the Truth.

Lov is infinitly Delightfull to its Object, and the
more Violent the more glorious. It is infinitly High,
Nothing can hurt it. And infinitly Great in all Extremes:
of Beauty and Excellency. Excess is its true Moderation:
Activity its Rest: and burning Fervency its only Refresh-
ment. Since therefore it containeth so many Miracles It
may well contain this one more, that it maketh evry one
Greatest, and among Lovers evry one is Supreme and
Soveraign.

    —Thomas Traherne, *The Second Century*

For religious conceptions have as their object, before
everything else, to express and explain, not that which
is exceptional and abnormal in things, but, on the contrary, that which is constant and regular.

       —Emile Durkheim,
    The Elementary Forms of the Religious Life

Anyone who has ever told the same story more
than once understands hyperbole instinctively: exaggeration serves to sharpen the narrative, to make it

more compact and distinct, to keep its listeners or readers attentive. Understood in this general way, hyperbole functions as an aspect of all literature, indeed, all creativity, by endowing art with the capacity to intensify, heighten, and impress. Understood more narrowly, however, hyperbole is a specific style that can be measured against the more ordinary or accepted conventions of artistic rendering. Some writers have called such flamboyant language "purple prose." The double meaning of the term purple is useful: it is both imperial and regal, demanding attention, and overly ornate, ostentatious, even marked by profanity.

According to Paul West's sympathetic explication, purple prose "suggests the impetuous abundance of Creation" by intensifying the imagination's knack for relishing the world. "The impulse here is to make everything larger than life, almost to overrespond, maybe because, habituated to life written *down*, in both senses, we become inured and have to be awakened with something almost invariably vivid."[1] Although such prose can stray into garish raptures, offering sudden inflations[2] that can devalue the author's intent, at its best it breaks the sacrosanct human bond to the ordinary and the banal. More like Latin American magical realism than North American minimalism, purple prose draws attention to itself in order to celebrate excessive energies which cannot be simply described or adequately contained.

The overwhelming phenomenon that was G. K. Chesterton is a legion of lessons in the many hued complexities of the color purple. Vivid and startling prose, pleated with images and overcrowded with examples, building its arguments on sudden rushes of odd analogies not propositions, leaping from the bold edges of one sharp depiction to the next, and yet sublimely unaware of its own intensity, a deluge of contagious claims as good natured as they are startling, as intoxicating as they are sober, Chesterton's breathless style is essentially polemical, a reductio ad absurdum taken to playful, not abusive extremes, a tendency to categorize everything without hurting anybody, a heroic prose in which at every moment something significant is held to be at stake. It is hearty, joyful, even jolly,[3] eager to reach the peak of a point but also willing to delay the whole ascent for the sake of a detour through barely relevant but entertaining illustrations, readily sacrificing efficiency for effect. Everything is fresh, as if we were reading pages not long after they had been written. Yet in the midst of this hyperbolic whirlwind, everything is meant to make sense, the extraordinary turns out to be the ordinary, the reckless is really the straight and narrow. Somehow, and this is the enigma I want to follow through Chesterton's works, hyperbole becomes understatement. Everything is more than what it appears to be, and yet appearances are just exactly what they seem.

Chesterton was a man who could write anything, and he did. He moved through genres like simpler souls move through the alphabet. It would be both impossible and senseless to read everything he ever wrote. Essays, journalism, novels, poetry, detective stories, literary criticism, social commentary, travelogues, drinking songs, philosophy, and theology rolled off his pen with regular ease and uneven brilliance. His prose breaks all the limits—mixing genres within a single work, muddling metaphors within a single sentence, moving rapidly back and forth between the sublime and the ridiculous, nonchalantly dropping paradoxes, and pointing out the obvious with great gusto—but it also denies its excesses by claiming to defend common sense, the ordinary, orthodoxy. His many wild and unruly visions, united by a sometimes annoying epigrammatic stylistic tic, were merely an attempt to see things as they already are. I want to argue that this dynamism—leading the reader on a wild chase that really follows the path home—structures all of Chesterton's most important works. It also raises the most crucial question about hyperbole itself. Does excess really fit? Is too much really only just enough? What is the power of a trope that claims to transcend, to over-whelm, to disorient, but really restores, placates, leaves everything the same?

From the very beginning of his career, Chesterton was a phenomenal force that puzzled everybody. A sur-vey of the reviews of his works shows that people were obsessed with his style.[4] Many were so struck by Chesterton's rhetoric that they could not imagine there was serious substance to be found there. His very bril-liance raises suspicions: how could something so clever be true? Chesterton understood his predicament, as this passage from his autobiography shows:

> If you say that two sheep added to two sheep make four sheep, your audience will accept it patiently— like sheep. But if you say it of two monkeys, or two kangaroos, or two sea-griffins, people will refuse to believe that two and two makes four. They seem to imagine that you must have made up the arith-metic, just as you have made up the illustration of the arithmetic.[5]

Even the explanation seems to be made in jest. He always seems to be enjoying himself too much to be credited with making a good argument.

Nevertheless, the arguments are there, too many to ignore or to analyze. Long before Karl Barth broke with liberalism in Germany in the famous commentary on Romans published in 1921, Chesterton had rejected lib-eralism in all of its forms, especially its facile optimism and easy belief in inevitable progress. As an alternative, he developed a unique postliberal theological project with a voice, like Barth's, laden with dialectical counter-point, denunciatory polemic, and twisted routes of argumentation. In Chesterton, however, these proclivi-ties are tempered with a distinctively English emphasis on the priority of common sense, a suspicion of intel-lectualism, and a use of vivid and colorful illustrations whose simplicity show no signs of Germanic convolutions. It is precisely from within this style, I want to argue, that his thought is to be found.

That his style is excessive is an observation always made but rarely analyzed in any depth or detail.[6] Perhaps the lack of specific analysis is due to the fact that hyperbole is usually not found in Chesterton in isolated statements; more often, it pervades all of his work, manifesting itself as a persistent enthusiasm, as if Chesterton is continually surprised at what he has to say. About such a general tone or attitude maybe only general remarks are possible. Nevertheless, it should be obvious that such a fundamental posture must be connected to an equally fundamental philosophical position. In his autobiography Chesterton insists that it is a primary wonder at the world as it is that drives his thought. "Even mere existence, reduced to its most primary limits, was extraordinary enough to be exciting."[7] In fact, it is ordinary existence, not, as with Flannery O'Connor, life at the edges, that Chesterton found so worthy of his gushing prose.

Chesterton linked this sense of wonder with his earliest years. He rejected the idea that childhood is a time of fantasy and dreams. "What was wonderful about childhood is that anything in it was a wonder."[8] To a child, facts themselves, indeed the entire world, seem miraculous. The world seems both concrete and vivid, simple and profound. This definite sense of reality is suppressed in later life.

> At the back of our brains, so to speak, there was a forgotten blaze or burst of astonishment at our own existence. The object of the artistic and spiritual life was to dig for this submerged sunrise of wonder, so that a man sitting in a chair might suddenly understand that he was actually alive, and be happy.[9]

All of his prose seeks to preserve "out of childhood a certain romance of receptiveness" to what he calls a common human mysticism.[10] As Ronald Knox has wisely observed, "he grew up from manhood into boyhood."[11] This wonder of the everyday gives to Chesterton's images a certain concreteness and matter-of-factness. No matter how wild his prose becomes, it is always in touch, almost literally, with the various objects and events that comprise the world that is immediately there.[12]

Chesterton himself did not think his capacity for wonder was anything remarkable. His instinct was always toward balance and moderation, even if his prose took him in other directions. From his own perspective, he could afford to rise to such rhetorical heights because he was so firmly rooted in down-to-earth concerns. "The very exaggeration of the sense that daylight and dandelions and all early experience are a sort of incredible vision would, if unbalanced by other truths, have become in my case very unbalanced indeed."[13] As he was fond of saying, the hero of even the most insane adventures must be himself perfectly sane. Otherwise, adventure would become chaos.

In fact, it is not only the concrete world that gives his visions referential stability but also, and more importantly, religion rounds off wonder with a sense of responsibility and perspective. "The notion [of wonder] was normal enough, and quite consistent with the Faith; indeed it was already part of it. But only as part of it could it have remained normal."[14] Religion makes sense of wonder, makes it part of a larger picture. The child says the world is miraculous; religion says—of course. This allows Chesterton to feel his sense of awe as a healthy, an appropriate response to life. "Existence is still a strange thing to me," he writes in the autobiography, shortly before his death, "and as a stranger I give it welcome."[15] The world that gives rise to such purple prose is seen to be plainly colored, even black and white, in the end. The wildest imagination that we could possibly exercise, Chesterton always seems to be saying, would really just see nothing more than reality itself.[16]

Chesterton is amazingly loyal to this basic insight throughout all of his works. One of his earliest books, first published in 1906, is a portrait of Charles Dickens that made Chesterton's name. He was accused, as with all of his studies of individual figures, of writing more about himself than Dickens; certainly the clarity with which he finds in Dickens this dynamic of hyperbole and understatement is uncanny. "Exaggeration is the definition of Art," he states and proceeds to uncover Dickens' own hyperbolic style.[17] Dickens' characters are wildly implausible—exaggerated—because Dickens loved them so much. In fact, Dickens was a great democrat who loved life and all of its possibilities. "Dickens overstrains and overstates a mood our period does not understand. The truth he exaggerates is exactly this old Revolution sense of infinite opportunity and boisterous brotherhood" (18). He too, just like Chesterton himself, has a sense of that primary wonder.

Hyperbole is a frequent topic of discussion; Chesterton often uses it as an explanatory tool. In fact, his longest and most explicit discussion of hyperbole comes in this book on Dickens. One key passage is worth quoting in full:

We feel troubled with too much where we have too little; we wish he [Dickens] would keep it within bounds. For we are all exact and scientific on the subjects we do not care about. We all immediately detect exaggeration in an exposition of Mormonism or a patriotic speech from Paraguay. We all require sobriety on the subject of the sea serpent. But the moment we begin to believe a thing ourselves, that moment we begin easily to overstate it; and the moment our souls become serious, our words become a little wild. And certain moderns are thus placed toward exaggeration. They permit any writer to emphasize doubts, for instance, for doubts are their religion, but they permit no man to emphasize dogmas. If a man be the mildest Christian, they smell "cant"; but he can be a raving windmill of pessimism, and they call it "temperament." If a moralist paints a wild picture of immorality, they doubt its truth, they say the devils are not so black as they are painted. But if a pessimist paints a wild picture of melancholy, they accept the whole horrible psychology, and they never ask if devils are as blue as they are painted. (18–19).

These are fascinating comments on a trope that is still today rarely analyzed with any insight. Hyperbole is easier to recognize in others than in ourselves. We especially feel troubled when we confront a hyperbole that magnifies something we lack. Moreover, social structures help to determine what is to count as hyperbolic in public discourse. Every system of beliefs is hyperbolically expressed, but the modern world is especially, and hypocritically, sensitive to the hyperboles of religion. The modern world defines religion as essentially excessive, that is, as superfluous, and yet the modern world completely, even deliberately misunderstands the nature of excess itself.

What makes Dickens's excesses so out of step with the modern world is his cheerfulness, according to Chesterton. In fact, Dickens reproduces the dynamism of an appropriate, a necessary excess that Chesterton thinks is so fundamental in life. "The essential Dickens' character," Chesterton writes, "was the conjunction of common sense with uncommon sensibility" (127). This is unusual: we like to think of the dull person who likes ordinary things mildly, or the extraordinary person who likes extreme things wildly. The genius of Dickens is that he liked ordinary things extraordinarily. Thus, his vision of the world was rooted in common sense—or at least a sense of the uncommon nature of common things. "He had the excess of the eccentric, but not the defects, not the narrowness" (129). The substance of his excesses were not idiosyncratic but were shared by everybody.

The modern world, skeptical and even cynical, would naturally only see Dickens's vision—as people now usually see Chesterton himself—as naive and old-fashioned. Yet Dickens' popularity with a great many people, if not always the literary critics, cannot be denied. "His books were in some ways the wildest on the face of the world," Chesterton exaggerates. Nevertheless, "He was an immoderate jester because he was a moderate thinker" (223). His extravagances made sense because he was only trying to express what everybody already knows. Indeed, Chesterton laments that today people think that you should not praise life too greatly: "We believe that you can have too much of a good thing—a blasphemous belief, which at one blow wrecks all the heavens that men have hoped for" (89-90). Certain exaggerations strike modern persons as unwarranted and shallow, and yet for Chesterton those same exaggerations can never go far enough.

Chesterton's two theological portraits—of Aquinas and St. Francis—paint these same features.[18] He often defended the Middle Ages, both politically[19] and theologically, and it is only natural that he was drawn to St. Francis's childlike obedience to the Gospels and passion for nature. Francis, in Chesterton's depiction first published in 1923, is the ultimate romantic who every moment exhibited an unbounded enthusiasm that gives life its due. Chesterton admits that not every enthusiasm is so proper: "There is some sort of enthusiasm that encourages excesses or covers faults."[20] Francis's enthusiasm, which was, certainly, rash and impetuous at times, represents a rebirth of religious fervor and joy after centuries of what Chesterton thought was a necessary but dreary Augustinian expiation and purgation. For Francis, life is an adventure in which everybody and everything has a special place.

To explain this vision, Chesterton talks about a broadening of the imagination that enabled Francis to act out of an "unconscious largeness" (48). Francis was like the troubadours, filled with love poems, or to be more exact, like the jongleurs, the counterpart to the more serious troubadours, jugglers, or jesters who pushed asceticism to such extremes that ironically they rediscovered the pleasures of living.[21] His counsels of perfection were a product of his optimism, not pessimism; he demanded a lot from his followers because he trusted them. Such counsels were "part of a particular vocation to astonish and awaken the world" (121). Indeed, Francis himself was continually astonished by the world: every event is dramatic, every gesture poetic, witnessed from a perspective imbued with an essential deference toward everything. Such loving humility, Chesterton seems to be saying, is the furthest reach of the religious imagination.

Such humility is also the common possession of most people; indeed, "his mysticism is so close to the common sense of the child" (88). True, his mysticism took the form of breaking worn and tired limits:

> All those limits in good fellowship and good form, all those landmarks of social life that divide the tolerable and the intolerable, all those social scruples and conventional conditions that are normal and even noble in ordinary men, all those things that hold many decent societies together, could never hold this man at all. (47)

Nevertheless, Francis, like Dickens, was not idiosyncratic. By breaking through the boundaries that separate people from people and people from nature, Francis expressed a certain abundant happiness that most people feel, even if only fleetingly. Thus, Chesterton finds a deep streak of common sense running through Francis's wild behavior—the common sense of wonder. Politics and theology are intermingled in this wonder: all parts of God's creation are good, and all people are equal. "His imaginative magnanimity afterwards rose like a tower to starry heights that might well seem dizzy and even crazy; but it was founded on this high table-land of human equality" (44). For an analogy, Chesterton talks about the nursery tale where a man bore a hole through the center of the earth and climbed so far down that at some point he began to climb up. Extremity meets—and in the encounter becomes—the ordinary.

One of Chesterton's first books was entitled *Heresies*, and even before he was very orthodox himself he was eager to point out where others stray from the truth.[22] In the book on Francis, he is eager to show that the saint himself is a loyal son of the church. "Every heresy," he writes, "has been an effort to narrow the church" (154). A heresy takes one aspect of Christian tradition and exaggerates it to the neglect of the whole. Heresies are, therefore, unbalanced and inappropriate hyperboles, and Francis ran this danger with his emphasis on asceticism. As could be expected, however, Francis properly proportioned his excesses to the beliefs of the common people he so dearly loved; indeed, "his very limitations make him larger" (151). The jongleur side to his personality preserves him from excessive excess:

> He was not a mere eccentric because he was always turning towards the centre and heart of the maze; he took the queerest and most zigzag short cuts through the wood, but he was always going home. He was not only far too humble to be an heresiarch, but he was far too human to desire to be an extremist, in the sense of an exile at the ends of the earth. The sense of humour which salts all the stories of his escapades alone prevented him from ever hardening into the solemnity of sectarian self-righteousness. (155)

Francis's imagination is so expansive that it is not in danger of slipping off to one side or the other. To broaden one's mind to such a wild extent that it becomes firmly rooted in common sense—bound to orthodoxy—is something most modern people cannot imagine.[23] Chesterton's instinct is that life on the margins—at the edges of extremity—moves to the center when pushed to its limits. If you climb down far enough, you can begin to see the world right way up again.

Chesterton's other theological portrait, a study of Thomas Aquinas published in 1933, was one of his most critically acclaimed books. His attraction to Thomas is not as readily obvious as his fascination for Francis; nevertheless, he really finds no essential differences between the two figures. He begins the work with a discussion of saints and hyperbole. The saint is a medicine, an antidote who is often mistaken for poison because the saint gives to the world what it needs, not what it wants. "He will generally be found restoring the world to sanity by exaggerating whatever the world neglects, which is by no means always the same element in every age."[24] The Victorian nineteenth century needed Francis because it neglected romanticism; the modern world, Chesterton is convinced, needs Thomas because it has neglected reason.

Reason, in fact, is the locus of hyperbole in Thomas. "Indeed, something in his character, which I have called elsewhere optimism, and for which I know no other approximate term, led him rather to exaggerate the extent to which all men would ultimately listen to reason" (38). By emphasizing the human capacity for rationality, pitting Aristotle against the Augustinian distrust of reason and will, Thomas affirms the goodness of the body and the trustworthiness of the senses. For Chesterton, this is not a problematical venture; reliance on Aristotle ironically makes Christendom more Christian. Affirming the embodiment of rationality enables Thomas more fully to celebrate God as the creator and the incarnate Son. Paradoxically, this same emphasis on rationality also does justice to the priority of revelation. Indeed, Thomas does not argue for revelation by arguing against reason, a move that for Chesterton would go against common sense. Instead, revelation complements and fulfills rationality, precisely because of rationality's search for ultimate order.

Exaggerating reason thus puts both the physical

and the supernatural in the proper perspective. It also restores a healthy order to the religious passions. In this sense, Thomas is the perfect counterpart to Francis. "A modern emotional religion might at any moment have turned Catholicism into Manicheanism. But when religion would have maddened men, Theology kept them sane" (110–111). This optimistic account of rationality, then, quickly turns into an apologetic for authority. "In short, a real knowledge of mankind will tell anybody that Religion is a very terrible thing; that it is truly a raging fire, and that Authority is often quite as much needed to restrain as to impose it" (104). Without the ordering activity of reason, Chesterton is suggesting, excess would dissipate; it would become deflated by its own impulsive energy, forced to run not across boundaries but out of control and into dead ends, with nowhere to go.

The themes in this pair of theological portraits are extended and deepened in what are arguably Chesterton's two greatest works, which also form a pair: the paradoxical and polemical *Orthodoxy*, published in 1908, and the more conventional and systematic *The Everlasting Man*, published in 1925.[25] *Orthodoxy* begins with the story of the English yachtsman who miscalculated and discovered England, thinking it was a new island in the South Seas.[26] The point is, as with all of Chesterton's works, to see everything as if for the first time—to be simultaneously astonished and at home with the world. Chesterton then admits—or claims—that he is that man. In fact, this book charts his own intellectual odyssey in which, oddly enough, the discoveries he makes in developing a personal philosophy on further investigation are found to perfectly coincide with Christian orthodoxy.

The conceit is a bit transparent and wearisome. How could he have known so little about theology to be so surprised that Christianity had already said the things he thought he discovered? This structural device, what amounts almost to a running gag in an oth-

erwise serious and at times profound work, does enable
Chesterton to exploit—and exhaust—the trope of irony.
The ironies, however, are too predictable: "When I fan-
cied that I stood alone I was really in the ridiculous
position of being backed up by all Christendom" (12).
Hyperbole, not irony, is Chesterton's strong trope, and
his mock surprise at having been anticipated by Christianity does not detract from his more central figurative
gesture, an encomium to bare existence. "It is one
thing," he writes, "to describe an interview with a gor-
gon or griffin, a creature who does not exist. It is
another thing to discover that the rhinoceros does exist
and then take pleasure in the fact that he looks as if he
didn't" (11). What is exceeds our imagination of what
might be.

Chesterton knows that the cynical world will not be
receptive to a voice strained with "painfully juvenile
exaggerations" (12). People try so hard to be reasonable,
without realizing that reason, taken to extremes, is
itself the problem. Reason, not imagination, makes people mad: "The madman is the man who has lost everything except his reason" (19). To seek an explanation of
everything is a sign of insanity; a sense of healthy complexity and ambiguity is better than logical complete-
ness. Ordinary people, Chesterton is convinced, understand this point thoroughly. In fact, "oddities only
strike ordinary people. Oddities do not strike odd people" (16). Mysticism, then, is more realistic than rationalism. "The morbid logician seeks to make everything
lucid, and succeeds in making everything mysterious.
The mystic allows one thing to be mysterious, and
everything else becomes lucid" (28). A little bit of
excess, and not too much, is necessary for a normal life.

Imagination alone, though, is not an adequate substitute for reason; religion puts the imagination itself
into perspective. Most people today, Chesterton suspects, doubt the truth, any truth, but do not doubt
themselves. Christianity is exactly the reverse: "If a man
would make his world large, he must be always making

himself small" (31). By exalting creation but chastising the ego, Christianity sets the imagination free. "All this gigantesque imagination, which is, perhaps, the mightiest of the pleasures of man, is at bottom entirely humble. It is impossible without humility to enjoy anything—even pride" (31). Only from the proper vantage point—the understatement of the self—can the world be understood and enjoyed as overwhelmingly great and good.

Chapter four, "The Ethics of Elfland," is perhaps the most revealing section of the book. Here he makes explicit what is contained in every one of his works. The visions of childhood, the myths and stories and fantasies that most people try to outgrow, are the most solid and reliable guides to life. "The vision is always a fact," he exaggerates. "It is the reality that is often a fraud" (46). Indeed, he boisterously claims that he learned all of his philosophy in the nursery. Fairy tales best express the mystery and wonder of the world.[27] "All that we call spirit and art and ecstasy only means that for one awful instant we remember that we forgot" (54). Chesterton accepts the world, though, not as an optimist but as a patriot, with a primary allegiance that does not preclude but instead encourages the desire for reform. In fact, these childhood tales do not just express wonder; they also implicitly articulate a theory of conditional joy. Wonder is possible only through limitations; humility, restraint, and thankfulness are its preconditions. Risk is a prerequisite for romance, duty for adventure.

So far, this sounds like a fairly coherent position; however, Chesterton wants to insist that it is really paradoxical. Theology makes contradictory claims—most basically, it is both optimistic and pessimistic—because reality itself is in contradiction. "It is this silent swerving from accuracy by an inch that is the uncanny element in everything. It seems a sort of secret treason in the universe" (81). Chesterton first came to the defense of Christianity, in fact, precisely because of all the contradictory criticisms people like Huxley and Spencer made against it. The critics go too far; people will use any argument against Christianity, even "swords that cut their own fingers, and the firebrands that burn their own houses...This is no exaggeration" (139). After reading such attacks, he decided that Christianity must have an odd shape, like a man who is both too fat and too thin; after all, Christianity was accused of affirming both timidity and (militaristic) courage, asceticism and the family, wrath and love, pride and humility.

Even after he concluded that Christianity was more sane than its critics, Chesterton could concede something to them: "There was really an element in it of emphasis and even frenzy which had justified the secularists in their superficial criticism" (91). The critics had discovered Christianity's essentially hyperbolic structure: in opposition to the Greek emphasis on moderation, the middle way, Christianity holds contradictory virtues together without watering them down to some tepid median. Christianity "separated the two ideas and then exaggerated them both" (94). Chesterton explains this dynamic in his typically vivid language: the Church "has always had a healthy hatred of pink. It hates the combination of two colours which is the feeble expedient of the philosophers" (97). The result is an ordered excess: while Christianity "had established a rule and order, the chief aim of that order was to give room for good things to run wild" (95). Like the cross, Christianity holds contraries together at right angles.

Everything fits together, though the balance is precarious. "Christianity was like a huge and ragged and romantic rock, which, though it sways on its pedestal at a touch, yet, because its exaggerated excrescences exactly balance each other, is enthroned there for a thousand years" (99). Orthodoxy is the perilous adventure that tries to maintain this balance through the definition of dogma. Dogma combines without dissolving contrary exaggerations. The result is not a metaphorical fusion but contradictions that converge in a complex whole. Heresies oppose dogma by taking one side of a contradiction and exaggerating it at the neglect of the fuller picture. Heresies are hyperboles that are out of control, disconnected from the cluster of excesses that comprise orthodoxy. "To have fallen into any of those open traps of error and exaggeration which fashion after fashion and sect after sect set along the historic path of Christendom—that would indeed have been simple" (101). The complex path of orthodoxy is also, in fact, the most radical path. Only from a fixed point, which is really the combination of contrary excesses, is progress possible. People need fixed ideals that balance extremes of both confidence and dissatisfaction in order to achieve change.

Chesterton's arguments scatter in many different directions in this book; his attack on liberal theology and defense of miracles is provocative and unsettling.[28] The one theme he persistently pursues, though, is the connection between religion and hyperbole. This connection, to return to my first chapter, is basically biblical. The style usually used to discuss Jesus, he says, perhaps wisely has been sweet and submissive, but the diction used by Jesus himself is curiously different, full of camels leaping through needles and mountains hurled into the sea. In Jesus, opposites are not fused together in some moderate manner but blaze side by side in a raging fire. The language of Jesus is essentially superlative. "The one explanation of the Gospel language that does explain it, is that it is the survey of one who from some supernatural height beholds some more startling synthesis" (147). This very language is the excess that orthodoxy seeks to preserve and maintain. "It is hardly an exaggeration to say that there is in historic Christendom a sort of unnatural life: it could be explained as a supernatural life" (149). The Christian tradition, by remaining the same, enables this language to work its magic, which is the enlargement of our visions to include something different, other. The Christian, in fact, "is always expecting to see some truth that he has never seen before" (155). Jesus' rhetorical heights beckon an unimaginable view.

Chesterton's own rhetoric becomes more careful, his arguments more controlled in *The Everlasting Man*, published in 1925 as a rebuttal to the evolutionary materialism of H. G. Wells's *The Outline of History*.[29] This work is actually his most polemical, but precisely because he has such a specific target, and a definite program of attack, his prose is less humorous and unpredictable. He begins the book by arguing that most of the critics of Christianity are petty and perverse in their criticisms; they are neither close enough nor sufficiently far away to have an objective view of the church.

> Now the best relation to our spiritual home is to be near enough to love it. But the next best is to be far enough away not to hate it. It is the contention of these pages that while the best judge of Christianity is a Christian, the next best judge would be something more like a Confucian. The worst judge of all is the man now most ready with his judgments; the ill-educated Christian turning gradually into the ill-tempered agnostic, entangled in the end of a feud of which he never understood the beginning; blighted with a sort of hereditary boredom with he knows not what, and already weary of hearing what he has never heard. (145)

Chesterton confesses that he would be "ashamed to talk such nonsense about the Lama of Thibet as they do about the Pope of Rome, or to have as little sympathy with Julian the Apostate as they have with the Society of Jesus" (147). To combat such unfounded prejudices, fighting words are needed.

The basic point of the book is that just as humanity is separated from nature by a sharp transition (as opposed to evolutionary theory), Jesus Christ is separated from humanity and thus Christianity is unique among the world religions (as opposed to the theories of comparative religions). Chesterton's arguments about prehistoric humanity and his descriptions of the decline of paganism are fascinating reading. On occasion, however, his sloganeering, which makes him so inimitably quotable, is too simple minded. "Man is not merely an evolution," he proclaims, "but rather a revolution" (158). He wants to emphasize humanity's mysteriousness, not naturalness. It is an unnatural exaggeration to see humanity as only a natural product, as animal. Yet it is not easy to describe what makes humanity different: "We must invoke the most wild and soaring sort of language; the imagination that can see what is there" (148). In fact, imagination itself is the commonplace that makes humanity unique.

The pagan imagination was in a sense very broad, or at least extremely tolerant and enlightened, but by trying to see everything it could not see the one crucial thing. "Exactly what it lost by these larger ideas is the largest of all" (227). Chesterton defines paganism as imagination unrestrained by theology; the church, by contrast, makes religion reasonable. Indeed, constraint and limitation are the preconditions of excess; successful hyperbole is bound to make sense. "The ultimate test even of the fantastic is the appropriateness of the inappropriate. And the test must appear merely arbitrary because it is merely artistic" (233–34). The mythology of paganism was a mere mood that was fated to die—an exuberance that could not last—and once dead it could not be resuscitated. Paganism spread its beliefs too thinly; its last burst of energy was channeled into hating the only thing that could replace it.

The wild notion of the incarnation concentrates all of the pagan desires for a human God into a single, strange story. In discussing the incarnation, Chesterton repeatedly returns to the language of excess. The critic, he notes, "laboriously explains the difficulty which we have always defiantly and almost derisively exaggerated; and mildly condemns as improbable something that we have almost madly exalted as incredible; as something that would be much too good to be truth,

except that it is true" (301). The point of the incarnation
is excess, paradox. "Bethlehem is emphatically a place
where extremes meet" (303). Henceforth, the highest
works only from below. The Romans who charged the
Christians with destroying the empire were closer to
the truth than those moderns "who tell us that the
Christians were a sort of ethical society, being martyred
in a languid fashion for telling men they had a duty to
their neighbors, and only mildly disliked because they
were meek and mild" (314). The incarnation, finally, is
as radical as a fairy tale: the king is discovered to be
serving in the ranks as a common soldier.

As in *Orthodoxy*, Chesterton portrays Jesus as an
essentially hyperbolic figure. He is certainly not a mild
and meek teacher. Even the great silence of the years
after his childhood and before his ministry is disrup-
tively excessive: "It is of all silences the most immense
and imaginatively impressive" (321). When Jesus did
speak, he always said more than could be imagined. His
style had "a singular air of piling tower upon tower by
the use of the *a fortiori*; making a padoga of degrees
like the seven heavens" (332). In analyzing the "how
much more" of the parable of the lillies of the field
Chesterton is himself reduced to exaggeration:

> It is like the building of a good Babel tower by white
> magic in a moment and in the movement of a hand;
> a tower heaved suddenly up to heaven on the top of
> which can be seen afar off, higher than we had fan-
> cied possible, the figure of man; lifted by three
> infinities above all other things, on a starry ladder
> of light logic and swift imagination. (333)

This proclamation of God's love for humanity is the
basis for the central Christian virtue, hope. "In Christendom hope has never been absent; rather it has been
errant, extravagant, excessively fixed upon fugitive
chances" (372). Hope can (must?) get out of hand, but it
errs in the right direction.

Even given all of his sensitivity to the trope of hyperbole, Chesterton still wants to assert that what Jesus said and was, although excessive, was not really exaggeration. This is especially true of Jesus' claim to be identical to God. "Why was this claim alone exaggerated unless this alone was made?" (334). The description of the impact of that claim, not the basic form of the claim itself, is hyperbolic: it is "a blow that broke the very backbone of history...and it steadied the world" (401). Indeed, "It is the one great startling statement that man has made since he spoke his first articulate word, instead of barking like a dog" (399). Chesterton seems to be a bit confused about the hyperbolic Jesus: is what he said true because it is excessive, or do we think it is excessive in spite of its being true?[30]

What role, in other words, should hyperbole play in understanding Christianity? Chesterton does almost apologize for speaking of Jesus in an extravagant mode, noting that his own style is "merely a counterblast to the commonplace exaggerations of [Jesus' alleged] amiability and mild idealism" (333). He is swerving from one extreme to another in order to correct the course of biblical interpretations. Even though he matches Jesus' hyperbole with his own, however, he does not recommend this as a general policy: "Every attempt to amplify that story [of Jesus' suffering] has diminished it" (340). What he is groping at is his own ambivalent attitude toward hyperbole itself; he wants to say that Jesus was and was not excessive, and that Christians should be likewise. "The mystery is how anything so startling should have remained so defiant and dogmatic and yet become perfectly normal and natural" (402). In the end, Christianity is only apparently hyperbolic. "I care not if the sceptic says it is a tall story; I cannot see how so toppling a tower could stand so long without a foundation" (402). In fact, "This madness has remained sane" (402). Jesus is, in the very last words of this book, "the lightning made eternal as the light" (403), a sharp and sudden, even terrifying illumination that becomes at

dawn flattened into the common occurrence of daylight. Chesterton has finally concluded his work: hyperbole has become litotes.

All of Chesterton's enthusiasms come crashing
down to this simple conclusion, the plain, even tepid
fact of affirming the goodness of existence. He has not
been exaggerating all along; in fact, given the wonders
of the world, he has been practicing understatement
instead. Rather, his exaggerations so fit the common
experience of life that only a cynic could think them
really hyperbolic. One of the most persistently hyperbolic writers of the twentieth century feels compelled
to deny that very trope. In his frantic effort to combat
paganism and to justify Christian faith, he risks betray-
ing his own most fundamental motif. His concerns in
the end are apologetical, not evangelical. He wants to
show that hyperbole, ironically, is hardly excessive at
all. That denial strikes at the heart of any understanding of this trope: is hyperbole that easy, does it really fit
our preunderstandings of the world, is it so simply
appropriate? Indeed, if the "too much" is always merely
"just right," does not hyperbole turn out to be irony—a
trope that pretends to be what it really is not? Is hyperbole really understatement in unnecessary disguise?

In a way, Chesterton's understanding of excess is
an important corrective to writers like Bataille and
O'Connor because it shows that this trope is not exclusively concerned with limit situations, where life is
experienced in extremis, at the point where the self's
world collapses and everything is possible. For Chesterton hyperbole is inhabited not only by those adventur-
ers who strive for the margins but also by those who are
firmly rooted in the everyday, an apparently stable center of habit and routine. Hyperbole is not about a particular kind of experience; alternatively, it is itself an
experience that can occur in any situation, no matter
how seemingly common and familiar. Even given life as
it always is, Chesterton is saying, life is more than we
can imagine, and that recognition can happen at any

time and any place. Nevertheless, Chesterton seems to move too quickly from the radical disorientation of a good hyperbole to its power to reorient. Some hyperboles, I want to suggest, can sustain this critical moment, when they go too far, and are not so easily appropriated and understood.

Perhaps the problem with Chesterton's prose style betrays a theological difficulty; his central excess is excessively affirmative and thus not sufficiently troubling. By connecting hyperbole to the wonder of childhood he unintentionally perpetuates one of the primary stereotypes of this trope. Joy, he thinks, not suffering, is the more fundamental experience of life.

> The mass of men have been forced to be gay about the little things, but sad about the big ones...Man is more himself, man is more manlike, when joy is the fundamental thing in him, and grief the superficial...Pessimism is at best an emotional half-holiday; joy is the uproarious labour by which all things exist...[Joy is] the gigantic secret of the Christian.[31]

His hyperbole, no matter how startling, always moves to affirm what he perceives to be a prior orientation; it does not seek to disturb or upset. This is why his prose can seem so repetitive; he is not really moving the reader anywhere but to where the reader already is. He would deny this fault, of course; indeed, he defines the saint as a hyperbole that negates, not affirms. "It is the paradox of history that each generation is converted by the saint who contradicts it most."[32] Even this definition, though, does not conceal how quickly he tries to defuse the impact of his claims; saints, in the end, are inimitably sane. They contradict superficial wants but satisfy basic needs. Figures of excess seen the right way put distortions into the proper perspective. Rather than developing the contemporary meaning of *religious* as zealous and excessive, Chesterton's work returns to the etymological meaning of religion as *religare*, to bind.

Religion goes too far only to bind us to what always already is. Purple becomes black and white; otherness becomes orthodoxy. Hyperbole takes the long way when a short cut would suffice.[33]

Some hyperboles, I have wanted to argue, clarify human experience only through contradiction, describe by disturbing—provide detours when there is no other path. Good hyperboles do not take the reader in a circle, ending where they began. Religious hyperboles, for example, beckon and promise, but they also warn and discourage. To follow an excessive discourse is to risk that it does not fit, is not appropriate, does not in the end make sense—rather, has its own sense, which defies the ordinary logic of life. Religious hyperboles promise a reorientation that occurs only through following the disorientation, the chaos,[34] to its very end, an end, of course, which can never fully be reached. Chesterton's prose does not fit into our world today because it too quickly says yes to life; it does not sufficiently sustain its transformative negation of all of our presuppositions that make the suffering of life too easy to ignore or evade. Since Chesterton's time we have seen too many excessive interruptions of history, of all of our values and ideals, to be drawn in by hyperboles that do not go, in the end, very far. To fit our feelings of despair and confusion, we need saints—figures of excess—who do not contradict our lives only to affirm life itself; we need something more negative than that, more troubling, and yet something that can be followed, even if we want to keep looking back. Good hyperboles give us a hyperreality that leaves us wanting ever more even as we inevitably learn to live with something less.

Chapter Six

Figures of Excess:
Going Too Far

I fear chiefly lest my expression may not be *extra-vagant* enough, may not wander far enough beyond the narrow limits of my daily experience, so as to be adequate to the truth of which I have been convinced. *Extra vagance!* it depends on how you are yarded. The migrating buffalo, which seeks new pastures in another latitude, is not extravagant like the cow which kicks over the pail, leaps the cow-yard fence, and runs after her calf, in milking time. I desire to speak somewhere *without* bounds: like a man in a waking moment, to men in their waking moments; for I am convinced that I cannot exaggerate enough even to lay the foundation of a true expression.

—Henry David Thoreau, *Walden*

All sensations of happiness have two things in common: *abundance* of feeling and *high spirits*, so that, like a fish, we feel our element around us and leap about in it. Good Christians will understand what Christian exuberance is.

—Friedrich Nietzsche, *Daybreak*

Not all excesses are equal. After all, the prodigal (wasteful, luxurious, rampant) son does return home, spent, exhausted, and ashamed (Luke 15:11–32).[1] After squandering his inheritance in purposeless living and falling prey to poverty and starvation, he turns home in expectation of judgment and the hope of being hired to work for food and keep; he is not, however, condemned—except by his moderate and self-controlled older brother, who comes back from the hard work of the field, not an exotic adventure in a far country. Indeed, the father meets his excesses not only with sympathetic understanding but also with an exorbitant banquet, a festive celebration that doubles and redeems his ruinous behavior. The opposition in the story is not between the two brothers, both of whom are unconditionally accepted and honored, but between the father and the sons. The story does not contrast rapacious behavior (the young son's lust for life) with parsimony (the older brother's persistence in the field, and his insistence that reward should be earned, deserved, measured). An excess that furiously spends everything is not, in the end, different from an excess that conserves and controls in order not to let go of anything at all. Instead, the story contrasts, to the dismay of all of the reasonable bystanders, an excess that squanders and an excess that clings with an excess that redeems. The father's activity is for *both* sons; voracious consumption and thrifty caution are two sides of the very same strategy of preserving and protecting the insecure and greedy self. The father displays—through the "maternal theme" of nourishment[2]—a giving for the other that heals and restores, not an unbounded consumption that flees or a sparing investment that calculates.

Clearly, the rebellious son is the model for Bataille's notion of purposeless acts of excess, while the prodigal's brother brings Chesterton to mind. Excess that is not directed toward the other risks becoming narcissistic and self-destructive; excess that does not go too far is not excessive at all. Jesus speaks a language similar to but finally different from both Bataille and Chesterton, placing impossible demands on the rich, promising the incredible to the faithful, honoring the gifts, the expenditures of the poorest of the poor, those who have almost nothing to give, disrupting the cunning calculations of the powerful in the name of something else. Jesus reverses the evaluations of the world (the first shall be last and the last shall be first) and offers an inclusive love that seems both impossible and ordinary, magnificent and just enough. "Lend without expecting any return," he is quoted as saying (Luke 6:35), promising not a reward of riches but a participation in the God who preserves all giving by granting the blessing of hope. Kierkegaard catches the ethical dimension, the justice of Jesus' extravagant words and deeds, while O'Connor preserves and recreates their wildness and unpredictability. Bataille goes too far and Chesterton not far enough; the point is to make the too far coincide with the just right.

Is such a project, to speak and act hyperbolically, possible today? To say and live hyperbole that is neither irrelevant nor predictable, neither absurd nor mundane, is, to speak in understatement, a difficult task. By going too far excess risks losing any connection with that which already is, and by trying to make sense it risks losing itself. To adopt a Wittgensteinian phrase, the bewitchment of hyperbole occurs when "language goes on holiday;"[3] the (dys)function and (mis)use of this most unordinary trope is, therefore, difficult to ascertain. From the modern perspective, the trouble is hardly worthwhile: excess is messy, uncontrollable, and naive. Hyperbole is a detour that might be temporarily necessary, given certain regrettable conditions, but for the impatient it is hardly convenient and certainly not praiseworthy. In order to stand out and slow its audience down, hyperbole decorates and embellishes that which can be stated more efficiently if one wants to get straight to the point.

The situation for hyperbole is more complicated, in fact, than simple rejection. For modern culture, hyperbole provides the material for and thus is always subordinated to the current trope of choice, irony, the ability to see things other than as they are, to turn things around, to show how events and actions and words achieve the opposite of what they intend. As one rhetorical expert has noted, "Nowadays only popular literature is predominantly non-ironical."[4] Irony is the mark of sophistication, the ultimate sign of the desire not to be deceived, the refusal to go anywhere or believe anything, let alone go too far and hope too much. Handled expertly, the corrosive effect of this acidic trope can accomplish the important specific tasks of undermining and disrupting unaware and hardened positions. Taken too far, irony threatens prematurely to limit and destroy visions that seek extension rather than dissolution: deflation awaits every inflation, one step ahead of any attempt to expand rather than reduce the imagination, anxious to betray enthusiasm's boundless trust in meaning and possibilities.

Perhaps the problem lies with the understanding and practice of hyperbole itself. Modern culture seems to be founded on the absolute division of the 'too much' from the 'just enough', a tension I have tried not to dissolve but to expose as essential to hyperbole's production of meaning. Most accounts of hyperbole take one side of the polarity 'too much' and 'just enough.' Either hyperbole cannot really be said, because the 'too much' is always co-opted by more of the same (hyperbole is always and really 'just enough' in the disguise of 'too much'), or hyperbole should not be said at all because it really does go too far, thus upsetting the precarious but necessary rule of prudence and common sense (hyperbole's 'too much' never coincides with 'just enough'). Two of the most important contemporary philosophers, Jacques Derrida and Richard Rorty, representing French deconstuctionism and North American pragmatism, typify each of these alternatives and offer instructive examples of the persistence of the Western rhetorical tradition on hyperbole and the insistence of the cunning of irony.

Derrida's sensitivity to rhetoric, especially the unconscious literary configurations of even the most abstruse philosophical texts, is well known. He is a master at showing the figurative basis of conceptual works, a rhetorical dimension that betrays the intentions of even the most systematic thought projects. His most developed comments about hyperbole come in a critique of Michel Foucault's attempt to rehabilitate the notion of madness in Western culture. Much of this essay, "Cogito and the History of Madness," involves a technical debate over a passage in Descartes that talks about madness, a passage that Derrida deftly connects to hyperbole. Hyperbole is the other of reason, and in the form of madness it is what reason must—but cannot fully—know in order to understand itself. Derrida argues, against Foucault, that madness never escapes the systems of rationality that define and deny it, and thus madness can never be isolated and described without repeating those very systems. "At its height hyperbole, the absolute opening, the uneconomic expenditure, is always reembraced by an economy and is overcome by economy. The relationship between reason, madness, and death is an economy, a structure of deferral whose irreducible originality must be respected."[5] Hyperbole as madness is always located in a set of relationships, a structure of differences that defers any essences and defies definitions.

Derrida warns us that any attempt to recuperate madness or appropriate hyperbole risks merely rearranging the very structures that have isolated these impertinent phenomena. This does not mean that Derrida does not believe in critique and suspicion; his own strategy is to disrupt metaphysical systems from within (by insertions and interventions that dissemble pure intentions and belittle stable origins) rather than from without. The combination of Derrida's methodological warning and his own strategies of insinuation and innuendo creates a critique of logocentrism that is nevertheless (ironically?) prejudiced against any effort to say, listen to, or name the other of reason. Contextualized in terms of rhetoric, irony, for Derrida, always circumvents hyperbole; that which tries to be more is always determined by—and eventually becomes again—that which

already is. Derrida's rejection of any form of transcendence or redemption, anything that tries to escape the
closure of Western metaphysics, is translated into an
antiecstatic rhetorical bias that makes irony the only
'real' trope. Hyperbole is reduced to the first movement
of irony, abbreviated and incomplete, a movement that
inevitably boomerangs when ironic reversal turns everything around.

One could also argue, in Derridean fashion, that
irony is actually parasitically dependent on hyperbole
for its manipulations and falsifications. Without a
hyperbole that really works, threatening a power that
could go too far, disrupting the control of reason, the
restrictive rejoinders of irony would seem superfluous,
beside the point. The attempt to organize and prioritize
the tropes, however, is ultimately a fruitless activity; it
presupposes an appeal to some basis that is, in the end,
extra-rhetorical, a basis that, according to deconstructionism, can never escape the boundaries of rhetoric
itself. Moreover, the attempt to rank the tropes does not
do justice to their relative autonomy, to the unsystem-
atic way they disrupt and interrupt each other, inter-
penetrating to create new and unpredictable shapes
and forms. In any case, Derrida does not make any
progress from the traditional Western philosophical
prejudices against hyperbole; on the contrary, his
attack on hyperbole can be seen as the culmination of
that very same tradition. Irony, the capacity to see not
further but more closely than hyperbole by showing
that all extreme claims really disclose the opposite of
what they pretend to mean, becomes the killer trope,
capable of deflating and defusing any discourse that
oversteps the boundaries that only irony itself, obsessively self-conscious, fully understands. Irony is a way
of staying on top, of being in control while Socratically
professing to know nothing, to merely be pointing out
what is really there all along, hidden to less dexterous
intelligences. Irony liberates by destroying.

Richard Rorty, one of the most influential contemporary North American philosophers, defends an all-encompassing pragmatism that debunks grand ideals, ambitious metanarratives, technical debates, and speculative dead ends in favor of classical utilitarian goals: increase happiness and decrease suffering without sacrificing a reasonable level of comfort for a broad section of the populace. His project even leads him to displace philosophy with literature, not because literature tells us more about language than philosophy but because it can help us to understand happiness and suffering better. The scope of philosophical labor is clearly limited: philosophy is not the world shaper and cultural organizer that most great philosophers have thought or hoped. Rorty gives philosophy a more realistic and modest aim. With the later Wittgenstein he thinks that philosophy for too long created unproductive pseudoproblems, and for penance it now needs to attend to the very real social problems that are alarmingly obvious and obnoxious.

This description belies Rorty's ambition. In a way, he wants to be the last philosopher, showing how Heidegger's talk of the end of metaphysics, Derrida's ironic reversals of philosophical jargon, and Dewey's commitment to social change as the criterion for successful thought all combine in his own work to create a modest defense of liberal democracy within which the philosopher acts to criticize and defame all those who take our attention away from the problems at hand. This program could open up new vistas for a philosophy of religion. The Cartesian search for philosophical foundations, for absolute cognitive certainty, first was supported by appeals to God and other religious beliefs but quickly forced philosophy and theology to part company, because the claims of the latter allegedly could not meet the strict criteria of the former.[6] However, if philosophy is not in the business of judging cognitive claims from some superior vantage of rigor and certainty, then religion can be treated on other grounds. The questions of a philosophy of religion would shrink in size but grow in importance. How has religion contributed to social change? How have religious beliefs and terms survived in the modern world and what role do they play? What kinds of languages are religious communities speaking today?

Anyone who has read Rorty will know that he does not envision these or any similar possibilities. Although he rarely writes about religion directly, his attitude is clear throughout his published works. It is an attitude, not scrupulously defended or constructively developed: religion is intellectually untenable, emotionally regressive, socially disastrous, and obviously obsolete.[7] His marginal comments about religion, many found in footnotes or asides, are of interest not only to the specialist in philosophy of religion. This slippage from a modest philosophical position to such charged and emotional opinions reveals not a contradiction but a clue to a prejudice that affects all of Rorty's work. Like Derrida, Rorty privileges irony over hyperbole. More specifically, Derrida's unstable irony, retooled for more specific goals, becomes in Rorty's work polemical satire, reducing the high and mighty to the petty and the absurd in the name of social progress. In practice, his basic rhetorical move is to restrict and restrain the scope of philosophy, reshaping big questions into small ones, showing that philosophers (and of course theologians) create problems that are not really there. Moderation, modesty, caution, skepticism—these are the invisible rhetorical boundaries that define his own discourse. Beliefs that go too far, that get out of hand, are subject to ridicule and abuse—to irony. In sum, Rorty's pragmatism is based on a clear demarcation of insiders and outsiders, those who can participate in his metanarrative journey away from the hyperbolic detours of extreme claims and unproductive visions toward the calm, cool seas of irony and those who get lost, mired in their own private dreams and fantasies.

Such defenses of irony should be taken to reflect their authors' own particular tastes and institutional situations; indeed, Derrida and Rorty both argue that there are no final arguments to be made in the area of rhetoric. Only metaphysics could pretend to have jurisdiction in this field, imposing one trope over the others, and not very many people believe in the power and authority of metaphysics anymore. In fact, irony belongs more to the cultured classes, the keepers of the academy, than to the great majority of people for whom all rhetorical gestures constitute unsettling departures from the tranquility of communication practiced as exchange and entertainment. Indeed, a rhetoric of moderation, flat, not hyperbolic and uninflected, not ironic, an antitropical discourse that seeks to deny rhetoric itself, governs the contemporary scene. The powers that determine not only *what* can and cannot be said but *how* anything can be said at all always resist being named, but they coalesce in that currently favorite word, pluralism, forcing upon irony the sneer of elitism and condemning hyperbole to polemic and outrage.

Denied the integrity of their own configurations, irony withdraws deeper into the academy and hyperbole tries to strike back. The melodramatics of fundamentalism in all of its varieties is the distorted expression of a resentment that an exclusive civility deserves but cannot apprehend. Moderation, legitimated and enforced by notions of civility and pluralism, forces hyperbole to sound ostentatious and crass.[8] To speak hyperbolically is to violate the fragile web of pluralism in which all views and all positions are made to hang together at the expense of the distinctiveness and singularity of any specific claim or demand. Judgment is sacrificed for the nourishment of toleration. As a general rule, the insidious rule of pluralism cannot be challenged—without the challenge appearing to be tasteless, awkward, and offensive.

To find the right tone for hyperbole is becoming increasingly difficult. If fundamentalists can sound acrimonious, others do not speak loudly enough to be heard at all. To belabor a point frequently made by theologians and sociologists, religions have become privatized by processes of modernization and secularization. Under duress, religions relocate their truth claims from the territory of publicly accountable and socially significant charges and demands to the space of interior desire and inward emotion.[9] As John Murray Cuddihy observes, today when people identify their religious affiliation they often use the phrase, "I happen to be...," a rhetorical ploy that denies further conversation about what must be at best a private decision or more likely an accidental state.[10] To the extent that religion is a public force, it is used to legitimate the ultimate concerns of tolerance and pluralism. As Cuddihy notes, the civil religion of the United States is a religion of civility.[11] Under the pressures of civility and moderation, Christianity has prepared the conditions that disallow its own most distinctive contributions. Agape becomes trust and respect, the demands of Christlike love are generalized as expressions of sociability and mutuality, belief is transformed into faith-understood-as-preference-or-taste. The power of love is turned into the capacity for everyone to like everything.

These comments about the social and institutional setting of Christianity's hyperboles raise some important questions. Does the social status of religion necessarily transform its hyperboles into a wholesale and reactionary polemic against and a disgruntled and alienated withdrawal from the status quo? How can hyperbole respond to but not be determined by the current social and cultural scene? I suspect that the chaos of contemporary culture provides reasons for hope as well as despair. Indeed, the fragmentation of culture, the increasing differentiation and specialization of every intellectual activity, the dispersal of belief systems by relativism and the frantic attempt to hold these systems cordially together under the rubric of pluralism (which the academy, abandoning the old line about the priority of rationality, now seeks to find its justification in upholding), all point to possibilities for rhetorical gestures that once would have seemed out of place. When it becomes clear even to those with Constantinian dreams of control and prestige that religion is marginalized, bereft of any easy access to the centers of power, sidelined and submerged by an arrangement that seeks pacification and constraint, then perhaps the religions can begin to find their voices again. In any case, the burden of religious rhetoric is to speak with a distinctive accent that is not merely a reproach to and thus dependent upon the dominant styles of the status quo. A hyperbole that obsessively rejects both moderation and irony will sound shrill and immature, thus confirming the prejudices of the tropes it wants to go beyond.

Does hyperbole have a voice of its own? True, hyperbole is always located in a situation, a context, an economy. It is always of something and toward something else. Christian claims about love, arguments about sacrifice and grace, Christology and eschatology, always occur within a horizon that helps to determine their form as well as their content. This raises the possibility that what is hyperbole in one situation may not be hyperbole at another time and place. What is hyperbole to me may not be hyperbole to you. Does religion 'sound' hyperbolic today only because of the rule of moderation, a taste for the ordinary and an aesthetic of the commonplace? Or is religion essentially extravagant and always excessive, regardless of social and cultural environment? Perhaps these are not the only choices. The ordinary can only be understood as such from a perspective that has already violated it. Excess is a necessary counterpart to the everyday. The expected and the extravagant take each other's measure but continually fail to understand each other in a ceaseless and unresolved dialectic. Religion always says something more, even though the form of that excess is inevitably codetermined by the social and institutional constraints that try to make it something less. Hyperbole is shaped by where it begins even as it always ends up somewhere else.

Perhaps the closest rhetorical analogy to religion in this regard is theater, where acting must magnify and accentuate—and thus be larger than life—but also disclose and describe—and thus be true to life. Religion in this sense is essentially theatrical, and it is no coincidence that the adjectives 'theatrical' and 'religious' both denote presumptuous and unseemly behavior. Phrases borrowed from the stage, like 'putting on an act,' 'making a scene,' 'stagey,' and 'exhibitionism,' are often used to criticize excessive behavior, while the charge of hypocrisy against religious persons is often merely an expression of an aesthetic of distaste for a rhetoric that necessarily oversteps its practical implementation and fulfillment. Both the actor and the believer must appeal to an audience's imagination of excess, and their messages are effective only to the extent that they subvert and replace the constraints of the everyday with condensed gestures that reverberate with an abundance and surplus of meaning.

Historically, of course, religion and theater have often been rivals,[12] but this is due not to opposition and contradiction but to similarities between these two worlds; only family resemblances could produce such heated denunciations and mean suspicions. Indeed, the religious critique of the theater, especially in its Puritan guise, often sounds like envy and resentment; the stage is competitively and successfully meeting needs religion has tried to monopolize. Both follow an impulse to turn hopes and fears into enduring realities in order to enact dramas of conflict and resolution. Furthermore, both risk relying on ritual and spectacle to portray worlds that are 'more than' and yet 'true to' the world as we usually know it. In any case, only when religion is reduced to ethics, to a rigorous moral code and an excessive sense of seriousness that have little to do with the love of the New Testament, can religion and the theater be taken as enemies with cross purposes.

In struggling for integrity, both theater and religion must combat the complacency and the reservations of moderation without merely counterbalancing everyday prudence with an exuberance that entertains without transforming, releases without challenging. There is, however, a difference between these two discourses of excess. When theater goes much too far it can only be charged with vulgarity and self-indulgence. When religion goes much too far the consequences are potentially much more disastrous. The lament and challenge that concludes Charles Taylor's magisterial book on the conflicts that comprise modernity deals precisely with this issue.[13] He agrees that the highest spiritual ideals of humanity—paths that pursue what he calls 'hypergoods,' goods "which not only are incomparably more important than others but provide the standpoint from which these must be weighed, judged, decided about" (63)—often have led as much to the slaughterhouse as to self-transcendence. Religion admittedly can be a poisoned chalice, and it has been linked to acts of all kinds of self-immolation and cruelty. Does this mean, though, that a sober, secular humanism should replace the excessive visions of religion? Taylor notes that the self-destructive and dangerous consequences of a spiritual aspiration cannot be taken as its absolute refutation. The good can always be perverted into evil. Moreover, something is lost when these deep and powerful metamundane drives are stifled. "Prudence constantly advises us to scale down our hopes and circumscribe our vision. But we deceive ourselves if we pretend that nothing is denied thereby of our humanity" (520). Should we give prudence the last word, or can we retrieve without overly taming those excessive visions that point to the something more that we always already are? Taylor ends his book with this dilemma, but he concludes on a hopeful, if oblique note. The question is fundamental: How far can we dare to go again, we grandchildren of the secular, scientific, enlightened mentality?

No matter what the situation, the words and deeds of hyperbole cannot be stifled for long. Obstacles and constraints only serve to magnify its power and effect.

Hyperbole is more than an occasional eruption or a useful tool. It is a basic fact of language and action that commands attention and warrants understanding on its own terms. An analysis of hyperbole, however, can offer more than rough definitions. It can also try to imagine what hyperbole would look like placed in the center of language and action, a hyperbole freed from the arrogant domination of irony as well as the stifling weight of moderation. This project would not only move further away from Western metaphysics than the privileging of philosophy's old ally, irony, but it would also demand a more comprehensive and radical rethinking of religion than pluralism allows. Can we today rediscover the hyperbole of the New Testament? Does the postmodern predicament—a disillusionment with disenchantment but suspicion of any "re's": rebirth, revival, reenchantment—bode only frustration and incoherence? As Paul Ricoeur notes, we have suffered through the desert of criticism, and we long to be called again.[14] Can we learn to speak a hyperbole that does not sound like bitter polemic and stubborn sectarianism? How can we find a way from hypercriticism— the droning labor of the academy—to hypervisions that can jolt us from our dormancy? Can we learn to recognize and follow figures, saints of excess, those who literally embody and express "an excessive desire...on behalf of the Other that seeks the cessation of another's suffering and the birth of another's joy"?[15]

Witness, for example, Simone Weil: the unbearable purity of her life is both intimidating and disturbing, but it demands as much as it resists understanding.[16] From the earliest age she identified wholeheartedly with the poor and the oppressed, and after years spent teaching philosophy and participating in trade union activities, she worked in various factories to understand better the nature of domination and power. These health shattering experiences, however, were not merely attempts to gather information; she always believed that to understand the forces of evil she had to identify, literally, with those who suffer. Indeed, her most intransigent instinct was to permit no rift between her ideas and her actions. Her trip to Nazi Germany, her participation in the Spanish Civil War and the French Resistance, her plan to organize and lead a front-line brigade of nurses during the war, her almost manic denial of any unnecessary luxuries or comforts, all attest to her scrupulous attempt to seek purity only through sacrificial actions of solidarity. She always sought the most difficult path, even when it inconvenienced others, but especially when it brought affliction to herself.

Such excesses are not easy to confront. At times, she does simply go too far; note, for example, her frequently unfair and brutal comments, echoes of Marcion, about Judaism, a by-product of her nearly Gnostic attempt to divide God into two, draining God of any humanlike motives or deeds and finding God's power only in powerlessness, strength in weakness. Note also her final act of suffering, in which her refusal to eat more than what the poorest of the French were eating got out of control and turned, according to some accounts, into her starving herself to death. Yet, for all of her contestatory ideas and vexing actions, never hesitating to put her principles into action, even in the most unsettling manner, she was always quick to show compassion toward individuals, not some abstract notion of humanity, and her thought was firmly rooted in practical, political concerns. Even her mystical experiences—listening for days to Gregorian chants while fighting numbing headaches, reading the poetry of George Herbert, contemplating the cross of Christ as the central mystery of Christianity—brought her closer to, not further away from, the suffering of others. Perhaps her most symbolically potent excess, her refusal of baptism even though she desired the sacraments so strongly, especially the eucharist—even in the midst of starvation all she really wanted was the body and blood of Jesus Christ, the suffering of God—is yet another sign of her rejection of privilege, of comfort, of any means of avoiding identifying with all those who are abandoned and forlorn.

Witness, for another example, Dietrich Bonhoeffer: Like Weil, he understood the danger of National Socialism from the beginning, and he abandoned his academic career in 1933 when Hitler took power. He left Germany for London, where he participated in the ecumenical movement, but returned to Germany in 1935 to help the Confessing Church and to direct an illegal Church Training College, which the Gestapo closed in 1940. Friends helped him travel to America in 1939, but he felt drawn to the suffering of his fellow Germans, and therefore he returned home, never regretting that difficult decision. In Germany, he was one of the leaders of a resistance movement that actively worked for the defeat of its own country, and he courageously pushed this organization forward even when all prospects for success seemed hopeless. Arrested in 1943, he ministered to his fellow prisoners, and his letters and papers from prison have become classic expressions of a hope that persists even though fully aware of its own impossible situation. By special order of Himmler he was hanged at the concentration camp at Flossenburg on April 9, 1945, just a few days before it was liberated.

Resulting in a starkly realistic assessment of German politics and an unnerving capacity for action against all odds, Bonhoeffer's theology is rooted in a literal, and thereby extravagant, reading of the Gospels. This is most evident in *The Cost of Discipleship*, first published in 1937, where he rejects what he calls cheap grace, salvation sold on the market like a common, useful good.[17] Cheap grace is what we give ourselves; it is Christianity without the cross. The price of cheap grace is the collapse of the church; true grace is costly in a different way. Indeed, "The only man who has the right to say that he is justified by grace alone is the man who has left all to follow Christ" (55). As he tirelessly repeats in this work, "Only the obedient believe" (70). Obedience precludes reflection; it is itself a kind of learning, but it is gained only through the suffering of loving action. "When Christ calls a man," he explains, "he bids him come and die" (99). Reading these words in the light of the subsequent course of Bonhoeffer's life makes their impact all the more incredible.[18]

Bonhoeffer knows that the Gospel—and his own discourse—is hyperbolic. To the terrible injunction about the offensive eye (see Matthew 5:27–32), he notes the dilemma it causes: "If we decide not to take it literally, we should be evading the seriousness of the commandment, and if on the other hand we decided it was to be taken literally, we should at once reveal the absurdity of the Christian position, and thereby invalidate the commandment" (148). He is not advocating a biblical literalism that would escape from the ambiguities of the world by finding a false solace in a pure and absolute text. Instead, he wants to direct our attention to the extravagance of Jesus' commands, an excess we are always much too eager to modify and defuse. He declares that the furthest reaches of the Gospel teaching is the commandment to love one's enemy, a "peculiar," "extraordinary," "more," "beyond all that" instruction. "No sacrifice which a lover would make for his beloved is too great for us to make for our enemy" (165). He does not want us to embrace the Gospels imaginatively and thus hypocritically. The only way to understand this hyperbolic discourse, Bonhoeffer is saying, is not through the understanding at all, but through action, through obedience, a life of redemptive suffering.

Finally, witness the growing attention to those whose voice theology too frequently has not heard, the witness of the poor, the marginalized, the outcasts, the anonymous, all those who do not speak the traditional language of academic theology and thus pose a threat to its canons of propriety, circumspection, and prudence. With the advent of liberation and feminist theologies, it is clear that theology is increasingly moving away from the aesthetic standards of the intellectual world in an effort not only to speak for but to listen to voices that do not fit into preconceived patterns of reflection and analysis. Theology from the underside goes over the top of traditional modes of religious problem posing and solving. Voices from beneath can sound shrill and strident; the temptation is to translate—quickly and efficiently—such exuberance into more reasonable modes of discourse. The insights and demands of the neglected, however, cannot be so easily circumvented; their forceful tone is too painfully clear. The poor, for example, constitute an excessive phenomenon not only in their numbers and suffering; they are also treated like surplus, like something useless and wasteful, irrelevant to the driving concerns of utility and production. Such marginalized voices can sound like nothing but mere exaggeration, which makes it increasingly crucial for all theologians to learn to speak hyperbole that is both challenging and inclusive, both demanding and broadening. I have become increasingly convinced that the irruption of these 'new' voices in religion can lead the way to the recovery of a biblical—an appropriate and yet exuberant—rhetoric for our own time.

Of course, it is always possible to reply, "Yes, but..." the classic retort to all exaggerations. Nevertheless, the "yes" reveals a fascination that the resistance of the "but" cannot completely extinguish. Indeed, only the tyrannical domination of the everyday and the ordinary keeps hyperbole from being more clearly recognized as an always present possibility in language and action alike. Kenneth Burke, for example, has argued that religion, serving as the ultimate test case for rhetorical theories, demonstrates a hyperbolic dimension inherent in all language: the tendency of words to transcend their nonverbal contexts. All discourses exhibit a logic of perfection in which words, which are to things as spirit is to matter, drive toward what Burke calls god terms, "a Title of Titles, a logic of entitlement that is completed by thus rising to ever and ever higher orders of general-ization."[19] Words stretch but never reach their intended objects; nevertheless, in that stretching language is liberated from any simple correlation confining word to object. "There is a sense in which language is not just 'natural,' but really does add a 'new dimension' to the things of nature (an observation that would be the logological equivalent of the theological statement that grace perfects nature)."[20] Language is funded by a desire for enlargement and expansion—to know more, say more, be more—that needs to be continually refreshed because it is ceaselessly frustrated.

Weil and Bonhoeffer show that this tendency toward transcendence in language can be embodied in individual histories as well. They are examples of that odd category that David Tracy calls the "mystical-prophetic."[21] Weil seems to be a kind of mystic, while Bonhoeffer's work displays a prophetic dimension, but the picture is more complex than that. Indeed, they belie any simple distinction between the meditative search for the dissolution of the self as it merges with what cannot be said (the mystical) and the proclamation of the judgment of the perfect word of the Other as both a diagnosis of and a cure for the mess of the human situation (the prophetic). In going too far—as with the mystics' disturbing claim to find the true self by losing it in a greater self, or relishing an abundant love in an astounding intimacy with God—they deliberately demand to be followed—as with the prophets' provocations that only obedience to the sweeping word of God can cleanse the structures of evil in order to create a new beginning. Their hyperbolic lives fuse together contemplation and praxis in an exemplary quest for purity that is also a manifestation of the ambiguity of human life, a complexity that nevertheless allows for real acts of charity and transformation. Hyperbole thus joins metaphor (the union with an other) and dialectic (the demand for deliberation, suspicion, and action).

Perhaps none of us can follow figures of excess like Weil or Bonhoeffer to the very end; most of us turn away from hyperbole at some point short of a full embrace. Such claims of purity have always struck religious communities as more than a bit heretical. This is the scandal, the insult of hyperbole that Chesterton's prose could not adequately reveal. For Chesterton hyperbole refers to what really is, rather than to what could or should be. The best hyperboles do not pretend to be descriptions but instead are prescriptive by offering adventures, not representations. Indeed, good hyperboles, as with Flannery O'Connor's literally endless stories, present bold departures even if they cannot promise a planned arrival. The "more" becomes what really "is" only through action, a wager that the added dimension will prove in practice to be necessary, essential—a blessed excess. The question, then, remains: through all of our hesitations and qualifications, can we learn to hear, to follow, even to speak hyperbole again today?

Most likely, we will fear to follow anybody today, to listen to anything. History has misled us so many times that we are right to be cautious. From common sense alone we feel the need to negate all of the easy solutions and facile promises that our culture spins around us. Yet we know that we cannot find truth merely from within, and when we look around, we see a world blinded to the suffering that we know to be so fundamentally unavoidable. We can never, as Paul Ricoeur has suggested, return to the first näivetés of our earliest dreams and hopes and ambitions.[22] We have been startled out of belief and hesitate to return to anything that smacks of innocence, but we feel an urge to move forward, to refuse to embrace the despair that lurks within all negations. Perhaps hyperbole gives us a second näiveté, in which we know we are being carried away, and we feel the danger of that flight, and yet we are willing to surrender—no matter how partially, or with whatever ironic reservations—to some vision of things that is more than what we find around us. Kierkegaard caught the subtlety of the doubleness of this trope during the last stages of his vitriolic attack on the Danish church: "The thing of being a Christian is infinitely high...Yet nevertheless it is possible for all."[23] Hyperbole's 'nevertheless' allows one to see the infinite without pretending that it is close up. There is no optical illusion because hyperbole does not lapse into fanaticism or literalism; like love, it sees everything clearly, sees even through its own enchantment without becoming disenchanted. It is a stretching that neither snaps nor loses its elasticity. Hyperbole—an impossible height absurdly clear, as close up as it is far away.

Can we dwell on such precarious peaks? Is Bataille right to argue that religion represents both the origin and the obliteration—by means of rationalization and utilization—of excessive acts of sacrifice and giving? Can excess be disorienting but not aimless, disordered but open to the other? Can excess be dangerous but also good, irrational but also true? Can communities foster and shape excessive acts of giving and caring without bureaucratizing and moralizing something the wider culture understands to be essentially private and personal? In *Blessed Rage for Order*, David Tracy defines the provenance of religion as limit-questions and limit-experiences, those situations—in science, morality, and everyday life—where the usual resources of existence are exhausted and fundamental questions arise that challenge every simple-minded assumption. In a limit-experience, horizons open up in uncanny and unaccountable ways, urging further reflection and action that transcend the expected and the ordinary. Religion, Tracy argues, provides a language that articulates the reference and context of such experiences. Religion represents—and names—the basic faith that limit-experiences both disclose and demand. Although Tracy talks about New Testament language in terms of metaphor, he often uses the language of hyperbole. Through strategies of intensification and transgression the sayings of Jesus respond to limit-situations by violating the ordinary with provocations and reassurances that promise healing only at the cost of excessive acts like renunciation and sacrifice.

The task of theology, then, is not to try to tame and control limit-experiences or to show how some of these experiences correspond to basic features of the human situation. Instead, theology should show how some experiences—taken to and across their limits—are appropriate responses to the claims and promises of the biblical witness to God's saving activity. The task of theology is to analyze—and even occasionally to speak—the language of hyperbole that both prompts and preserves experiences in which limits are broken and yet life is (mysteriously and hopefully) sustained and enhanced.[24]

The implications for the central problem of theology—which concerns the extravagance, as Chesterton understood, of not only the parables but also the person of Jesus Christ—are diverse but clear. Christology must do justice to the amazing claim of the incarnation. Neither the traditional two natures doctrine nor the liberal reduction of Jesus to a great moral teacher and example adequately respond to the dynamic and explosive unity of Jesus Christ, who is, after all, a relationship, not a representation. The structure of this relationship—like all unpredictable movements—is difficult to describe. In Jesus Christ the Christian recognizes an excess that breaks the boundaries of the ordinary in order to initiate, enhance, and sustain reciprocal acts of self-denial and self-donation. The relationship between God and humanity in Jesus Christ is not an exchange—a barter, the payment of debts, an investment in the future. Moreover, the drama of Jesus Christ should not be conceptualized in terms of a placating or expiatory sacrifice. Christians find in Jesus Christ a gift that itself keeps giving, no matter what the cost. It is a gift that does not demand repayment but instead opens up a space where the risk of giving can be recognized as the reception of the other. God's unbounded gift to us through Jesus Christ establishes God's humanity; we give to others to find ourselves. Such giving is not the by-product of violent self-punishment. It is also not the sentimental and magical expectation of the proportionate and compensatory return of every gift. The excess of sacrifice seeks mutual recognition through celebrating the difference and the integrity of the other. Jesus Christ empowers our capacity for generosity, for the hope that through the other we can find the self. The self is the final gift, what is gracefully left over from the act of giving, what remains at the end of sacrifice.

What can we hope today? Do we trust yet one more proposal for reform, one more argument about change, one more plan that will, no doubt, be quickly co-opted by the status quo? More importantly, how can we hope for anything at all when we fear being caught affirming something that will only prove to be an illusion, a deception? How can we ask others to trust and accept our own giving when we know our all-too-human selves only too well? How can we receive when we do not even know how to give? Is there any basis for hope in all that we are, in all that we see and do? Only the sensational seems plausible, only the uncommon makes sense. Only too much—and not even that—is enough.

Epilogue

Peer Gynt, in Henrik Ibsen's play of the same name, a play impossible to summarize due to its shifting styles and its ebullient tone, tells a tale, after returning home from many strange travels, about a scene in San Francisco in which mountebanks and charlatans are performing their various sly talents. One day, Gynt relates, the Devil decides to join the fun. His trick is to squeal like a pig, and what the audience does not know is that he hides a real pig beneath his cloak, pinching it when he himself pretends to be grunting. After the pig screeches (the pig is actually killed in the process), the Devil bows and departs, leaving the experts to judge the performance. "Some found the tone of the squeals too thin. Others thought the death-shriek a trifle affected. But on one point all were agreed. The actual grunting had been, throughout, decidedly exaggerated. So the Devil got his due; a just reward for over-estimating the intelligence of his audience." (Henrik Ibsen, *Peer Gynt,* trans. Michael Meyer [New York: Anchor Books, 1963], 132.) The stage direction notes that the crowd listening to Gynt falls into an uncertain silence as Gynt likewise bows and departs. His parable, it is true, is difficult to fathom. Peer Gynt is, after all, a great exaggerator, and it is tempting to inquire, upon hearing this story, what pains and sufferings he himself is concealing.

In the world of theater, this story is frequently taken as a warning against a certain kind of hyperrealism, perhaps what is often called melodrama, that seeks to display the pain and suffering of life without the mediation of artistic method and the control of dramatic purpose. People do not want too much reality in their art; they need both distance and distortion, both

craft and manipulation. A style that too eagerly and literally approaches the real thing, sacrificing form to
content, can appear to be too forceful, too dramatic—in
sum, excessive. In art, reality itself can appear completely unreal. The irony here is that the Devil hoped to
win praise by his verisimilitude and instead earned critique by the same measure.

On a broader note, Gynt's story is also about the
dangers of mistaking the real thing for playful artifice.
The Devil transforms the awful sounds of suffering into
the language of spectacle and fantasy and is met with
neither applause nor anger but aesthetic analysis and
disbelief. If the Devil meant to amuse the crowd by
claiming the pig's pained voice as his own, he failed his
trick but still succeeded in obscuring the method of the
magic. His trick worked too well: the critics refused to
acknowledge what they actually heard and instead
blamed the Devil for an exuberantly crude imitation.
There is a lesson here, then, not only for performers but
for audiences as well. This story, in fact, can serve as a
metaphor for the way in which audiences use exaggeration to deflate that which is stubbornly unbearable and
gratingly vivid. In the stories we tell each other we do
not want to believe what we know is all too real; we
would rather imagine that what we hear is fantastic,
incredible, and, thus, illusory. Ironically, when the truth
is really too much, the charge that the truth is exaggerated can appear to be just right. Moreover, people want
even their exaggerations in small doses, slight distortions that give of the truth in suggestively indirect ways,
creating a healthy distance between reality and effect.

One possible moral of this tale, then, is that in
cases like this, the reality has more power than any
expression could ever achieve. Simply put, not all realities lend themselves well to exaggeration; some objects
rightfully resist aesthetic heightening and figurative
emphasis. Authentic suffering, for example, cannot be
appropriately exaggerated. Yet sometimes we must
speak for the suffering of others, relying on their very

own voices, and sometimes we must speak directly, putting the unwelcome into words; sometimes shrieking like a pig is the most proper thing to do. The risk involved is enormous. To speak the stark truth can be perceived as going too far when everybody else is straining to hear that which only slightly deviates from the ordinary and the everyday. When we hazard exclamations that nonetheless are not exaggerations, we must be willing to incur the consequences that people do not want the real thing, but drama and indirection instead. Sometimes the plain truth is too much when people expect something more in its addition. In fact, even when rhetorical modesty and reserve prevails, people desperately and eagerly want to hear exaggerations where none exist, that is, when the truth is all too troubling and overwhelming.

The subtle lessons here for hyperbole—from a tale in which no exaggeration occurs—concern its abuse and misuse. Nevertheless, hyperbole is not always feigned insincerely or imposed as a defensive interpretive strategy. To return to my own contribution to a theory of hyperbole, perhaps it is helpful to remark on the simplest instance of this trope's use. When something that is known to be true regardless of its expression is exaggerated, we can look for the reason why this trope was employed by examining the context of the speech act, and we can measure the impact of this figure by comparing it to the actual object itself. We have, in other words, means other than hyperbole to understand what the hyperbole is trying to do. In other cases, I have wanted to argue, there is an even more complex relation between reality and exaggeration, between truth and trope. Indeed, it is not uncommon to sense that a statement or an entire discourse is exaggerated and yet not be able to say what it is that has been extended and amplified.

The best exaggerations so alter the way we perceive their referents that we can no longer draw a clear line between the hyperbole and more ordinary modes of description. Hyperbole can be literally descriptive of an object we might not otherwise adequately know or understand. This is the case, I have claimed, with much religious discourse. It pushes the talk about God, love, and hope to such extremes that we are hardly able anymore to separate the expected from the extraordinary. We can no longer distinguish between the reality that religious discourse is *about* and the reality that such discourse *creates.* With religious language, the reality it represents is far from being clearly accessible by other means. Hyperbole, then, is not a transparent trope; sometimes the excess itself partakes of that which it expresses. The exaggeration of love does not conceal some lesser reality beneath an unnecessarily embellished discourse. Religious language does not merely blow out of proportion what everybody already knows anyway. Religious hyperboles do not obscure or hide; they reveal. In theological terms all I am suggesting is the following: The Word of God speaks into being the love it creates with a style appropriate to its mission, and we in turn believe what we cannot see but what we can say.

Notes

Chapter 1.

1. The essay is published in Sheldon Sacks, ed., *On Metaphor* (Chicago: University of Chicago Press, 1979).

2. There are theological as well as rhetorical reasons for Tracy's limitation. Tracy's irenic pluralism—his attempt to draw together all perspectives on any particular topic without denigrating each perspective's autonomy—does not allow him to follow any one perspective to its (il)logical conclusion. In other words, hyperbole is by definition excluded from his otherwise comprehensive analogical imagination. However, his interest in the classic as an excessive phenomenon (defined as carrying a surplus of meaning) and his many analyses of religion as responding to limit or extreme situations point to his own dependence on hyperbole. Note the following from *Plurality and Ambiguity* (San Francisco: Harper and Row, 1987): "My own theology of religious classics...needs to suspect its predilection for extremities and intensifications" (97) which tends to downplay "the vast undertow of ordinary people leading ordinary religious lives" (96). Nevertheless, Tracy insists on an analogical imagination, which envisions the different as possible, not a hyperbolic imagination, which sees the different as impossible and yet somehow necessary.

3. Martin Ostwald, trans., *Nicomachean Ethics* (Indianapolis: Bobbs-Merril, 1962), 47. Also see pp. 104–9.

4. See Longinus, *On Great Writing*, trans. G. M A. Grube (Indianapolis: Hackett, 1991). Grube's introduction provides a good discussion of the problematic authorship and dating of this work. It probably dates from either the first or third century C.E.

5. At one point in the treatise, in a discussion of Plato, Longinus provides a broad, philosophical account of the desire for excess: "That is why the whole universe gives insufficient scope to man's power of contemplation and reflection, but his thoughts often pass beyond the boundaries of the surrounding world. Anyone who looks at life in all its aspects will see how far the remarkable, the great, and the beautiful predominate in all things, and he

will soon understand to what end we have been born" (47). Hyperbole points the way toward the majestic wellsprings of life.

6. Quoted from James J. Murphy, *Rhetoric in the Middle Ages* (Berkeley: University of California Press, 1974), 370.

7. Quintilian, *On the Teaching of Speaking and Writing*, trans. James J. Murphy, ed. (Carbondale: Southern Illinois University Press, 1987), 11.5.11; 108–9.

8. Ibid., 2.3.8; 96.

9. Quintilian, *Institutes of Oratory*, trans. H. E. Butler (Loeb Library, 1921), 8.6.67; 339.

10. Ibid., 8.6.74; 343.

11. Seneca, *De Beneficiis*, 7.22.1–7, 23.2; *Moral Essays*, trans. J. W. Basore (Loeb Library, 1935), III, 508–11.

12. Butler translation, 8.6.77; 343.

13. Augustine, *On Christian Doctrine*, trans. D. W. Robertson, Jr. (Indianapolis: Bobbs-Merrill, 1958).

14. Calvin, *Institutes of the Christian Religion*, vol. 1, trans. Ford Lewis Battles, ed. John T. McNeill (Philadelphia: Westminster, 1960), 13 (from the prefatory address to King Francis).

15. Paul Ramsey, *Basic Christian Ethics* (New York: Scribner's, 1950), 194. The passage that follows this quote is illuminating: "The classic and Renaissance ideal of moderate and well-rounded human activity, and the Romantic ideal, so well exemplified by Goethe, of never fixing upon any single moment in experience as if it were enough without something of all the other possibilities going to make up a full life—these must be subjected to radical revision before being baptized Christian. This can be seen in the single instance of Albert Schweitzer: Which as Christians do we admire more, the world of learning, music and art he carries on his shoulders, or the triumph in him of Jesus' ethic of the extreme? Which makes him more mature, more truly a man, moderation or immoderation? While undoubtedly he comes close to being admirable in every respect, the question may still be raised whether the distinctively Christian thing about this man Schweitzer consists in what he has been able to include or what, without having to, he has been able to exclude" (194). Note that Ramsey tends to equate the Aristotelian, or Apollonian side of Greek culture—while neglecting the excessive strains, the Dionysian—with the whole of Greek thought. For a representative Greek comment on the limits of excess, note

the following from the Chorus in Euripides' *Medea*: "Love may go too far and involve men in dishonor and disgrace. But if the goddess comes in just measure, there is none so rich in blessing...May moderation content me, the fairest gift of Heaven." From *Ten Plays*, trans. Moses Hadas and John McLean (New York: Bantam Books, 1960), 46.

16. Ibid., 226. Following Augustine, Thomas Aquinas also celebrates excess only when—in the forms of faith, hope, charity—it is directed toward God, because "It is not possible to sin by excess with respect to God, the object of theological virtue." From *Summa Theologiae*, I–II, Question LXIV, Article 4. Although both Augustine and Aquinas encourage excess, they also compartmentalize it by relegating it to the spiritual realm. Aquinas especially risks preserving the centrality of prudence, which strictly governs the intellectual and moral virtues even though it finds completion in the extravagant virtue of love.

17. I realize that my abbreviated account of the trials of hyperbole leaves out the Middle Ages; for interesting comments in this regard, especially focusing on medieval panegyric, see Ernst Robert Curtius, *European Literature and the Latin Middle Ages*, trans. Willard R. Trask (New York: Pantheon, 1953), 159–66. Also see Jean Leclerq, *The Love of Learning and the Desire for God*, trans. Catharine Misrahi (New York: Fordham University Press, 1982), 131–33. Note Leclerq's comment, in a discussion of Peter Damian: "The holiest are the ones who exaggerate the most because their zeal is the most ardent (one might dare say the 'most violent' in the sense used in the Gospel which says that the violent take the kingdom of God by storm)" (132). Leclerq, though, understands exaggeration only as emphasis or magnification. The transition from the ancient world to medieval Christendom is probably the most important period for a history of hyperbole, but my brief sketch cannot do justice to such a prolonged and complicated social transformtion. By focusing on philosophical prejudices against hyperbole, I have risked ignoring the importance of excessive acts in Greek and Roman religion as well as other cultural spheres. By adopting Greek philosophy but not Greek religion, Christian theologians tended to perpetuate the ancient prejudice against excess; however, the Christianization of the Roman world is not so simple. Medieval Christianity valued excess in many ways, from the rhetoric of the Crusades to the zeal of asceticism, from the lyricism of the mystics to the political claims of the papacy. I will deal with the relationship between Christianity and paganism indirectly through a discussion of the attitudes of Bataille and Chesterton. Both find these two religions to be in opposition precisely on the issue of exccess: Bataille

wants to return to pagan excess as opposed to Christian morality, and Chesterton finds in Christian excesses a sustaining power and moral sensibility that paganism lacked. Bataille blames the Protestant Reformation, not medieval Christendom, for the decline of excess, while Chesterton's piety is polemically medieval. I am most interested in a set of philosophical and rhetorical prejudices that do affect as well as reflect social practice and seem remarkably consistent from the ancient world through the Enlightenment to today.

18. William C. Placher, *A History of Christian Theology* (Philadelphia: Westminster, 1983), 244.

19. Gerald R. Cragg, *The Church and the Age of Reason* (New York: Penguin, 1967), 15.

20. Discussed in Chaim Perelman and L. Olbrects-Tyteca, *The New Rhetoric*, trans. John Wilkinson and Purcell Weaver (New York: Notre Dame, 1969). For a fascinating critique of Du Marsais, see Tzvetan Todorov, *Theories of the Symbol*, trans. Catherine Porter (Ithaca: Cornell University Press, 1982), chapter 3.

21. Brian Vickers praises Priestley's approach to hyperbole in his essay, "The 'Songs and Sonnets' and the Rhetoric of Hyperbole," in *John Donne, Essays in Celebration*, ed. A. J. Smith (London: Methuen, 1972), 132–74. Although I disagree with Vickers's reading of Priestley, I have learned much from this essay, especially its brief history of theories of hyperbole in the English Renaissance. My quotations from Priestley are from the facsimile printed by Scholars Press Limited, Menston, England, 1968. It is interesting that Priestley's understanding of rhetoric is not unrelated to his other scholarly projects. In his Christology, for example, he minimizes the uniqueness of Jesus by comparing him, favorably, to Socrates, concluding that revealed religion enlarges but does not alter the storehouse of moral wisdom of humankind. For a brief discussion of Prietley's *The Corruptions of Christianity, A Harmony of the Gospels*, and *Socrates and Jesus Compared*, see Jaroslav Pelikan's analysis of the image of Jesus as a teacher of common sense in *Jesus through the Centuries* (New Haven: Yale University Press, 1985), 189.

22. Note Johnson's criticisms against Cowley and the other metaphysical poets in *Lives of the English Poets*, vol. 1, ed. George Birkbeck Hill (Oxford: Clarendon Press, 1907): "What they wanted however of the sublime they endeavored to supply by hyperbole; their amplification had no limits: they left not only reason but fancy behind them, and produced combinations of confused magnificence that not only could not be credited, but could not be imagined" (21). Nevertheless, "they likewise sometimes struck out unexpected

truth: if their conceits were far-fetched, they were often worth the carriage" (21). In an essay on Butler he displays the root of his prejudice against excess: "All disproportion is unnatural; and from what is unnatural we can derive only the pleasure which novelty produces. We admire it awhile as a strange thing; but when it is no longer strange, we perceive its deformity" (218). In the *Rambler*, no. 137, Johnson explains his rather prosaic understanding of the sublime that underlies these cautions and hesitations: "Wonder is a pause of reason, a sudden cessation of the mental progress, which lasts only while the understanding is fixed upon some single idea, and is at an end when it recovers force enough to divide the object into its parts, or mark the intermediate gradations from the first agent to the last consequences." *The Works of Samuel Johnson*, vol. 3 (London: Bentley, 1823), 417.

23. Louis Wirth Marvick, *Mallarme and the Sublime* (Albany: SUNY Press, 1986), 19.

24. See Robert Evans, "Hyperbole," in the *Princeton Encyclopedia of Poetry and Poetics*, ed. Alex Preminger (Princeton: Princeton University Press, 1965).

25. My comments about the danger or the challenge of the supplement are derived from Jacques Derrida, *Of Grammatology*, trans. Gayatri Chakravorty Spivak (Baltimore: The Johns Hopkins University Press, 1976), especially 158–59. For commentary, see Jonathan Culler, *On Deconstruction* (Ithaca: Cornell University Press, 1982), 102–6. Hyperbole can be reduced to a supplement understood as mere addition only if discourse is construed in idealistic terms as the pure and disinterested exchange of content.

26. For a good argument that excess is the most fundamental figure in the contemporary world, see Allen S. Weiss, *The Aesthetics of Excess* (Albany: SUNY Press, 1989).

27. Robert J. Fogelin, *Figuratively Speaking* (New Haven: Yale University Press, 1988), 13.

28. It would probably be more technically accurate to call litotes the contrast, not opposite of hyperbole. A good hyperbole cannot be deflated, domesticated, or neutralized by understatement simply by the addition of a negative, although understatements themselves are frequently expressed with a negative. The relationships among the various tropes is complex and can only be partially explained with the use of labels and distinctions. Take these various examples concerning someone running very quickly: Hyperbole: He was doing ninety. Hyperbole mixed with simile: He was running like the wind. Hyperbole mixed with metaphor: His

lightning bolt dash...Hyperbole deflated by litotes: He was not even moving. Note that the litotes counters the hyperbole without completely denying it, because the litotes also does not mean what it says. In fact, the litotes, in this example, is very close to irony, which says the opposite of what is meant. My point about the relationship between hyperbole and litotes is that excessive claims can lead to their practical opposite as a strategy of refusal and resistance. The litotes, for example, can be an ironic response to hyperbole, a way of showing that the hyperbole is recognized for what it is and countered with a statement that says nearly the same thing in a different, less aggressively extravagant form. Thus, the litotes does not necessarily contradict the hyperbole, and it is not correct to call it the hyperbole's opposite, although it does serve as a contrast to the hyperbole that can function to reject, correct, or even continue the original excess. As Perelman and Olbrechts-Tyteca explain, "The function of hyperbole is often to prepare for litotes, the purpose of which might otherwise be missed." *The New Rhetoric*, 292.

29. Speaking at a critical distance from religion, Albert Camus understood this point better than many people living within religious belief: "The only possible dialogue is the kind between people who remain what they are and speak their minds. This is tantamount to saying that the world of today needs Christians who remain Christians...What the world expects of Christians is that Christians should speak out, loud and clear, and that they should voice their condemnation [of evil] in such a way that never a doubt, never the slightest doubt, could rise in the heart of the simplest man." From "The Unbeliever and Christians," in *Resistance, Rebellion, and Death*, trans. Justin O'Brien (New York: Random House, 1960), 70–71. For his own analysis of the relationship between moderation and excess, see *The Rebel*, trans. Anthony Bower (New York: Vintage Books, 1956), 294–301.

30. Adolf von Harnack, *What is Christianity* (Philadelphia: Fortress, 1986), p. 28.

31. Claude Cicero Douglas, *The Use of Hyperbole in the New Testament* (Ph.D. diss., University of Chicago, 1925).

32. G. K. Chesterton, *Orthodoxy* (New York: Doubleday, 1936), 146. I will return to this observation in the chapter on Chesterton.

33. James Gustafson, *Ethics from a Theocentric Perspective*, vol. 1, *Theology and Ethics* (Chicago: University of Chicago Press, 1981), 202–3.

34. James Gustafson, *Can Ethics Be Christian?* (University of

Chicago Press, 1975), 67. Note another important comment about hyperbole in *Theocentric Ethics*: "To question the biblical claim that all things are or will be made new in Christ, to see such a claim as hyperbole, is not to deny that 'newness' is possible, that what now exists for man can be surpassed, or that there are conditions for hoping. To construe man in this theocentric perspective does require that aspirations be tempered by what we know of our place in the universe" (310–11). Gustafson wants people to enlarge their religious imaginations by thinking of God as concerned with the whole of things, not just with human beings. Ironically, the price he pays is a constriction of the biblical discourse that he rightly labels hyperbolic.

35. For another analysis of the phrase "God is love," from the perspective of process theology, see the exchange between Schubert Ogden and Charles Hartshorne in John Cobb and Franklin Gamwell, eds., *Conversations with Charles Hartshorne* (Chicago: University of Chicago Press, 1984), 16–42. Process thought strongly affirms the love of God, but it focuses on conceptual clarification, for example, the question of levels of language, the relationship among analogy, literal and metaphysical statements. While all theologians can learn from these debates, process thinkers tend to neglect the primary power to manifest a suprarational truth that some language—hyperbolic discourse—expresses. In other words, they move too quickly from the poetic to the conceptual and metaphysical.

36. John H. Yoder in *James M. Gustafson's Theocentric Ethics: Interpretations and Assessments*, Harlan R. Beckley and Charles M. Swezey, eds. (Macon, Ga.: Mercer University Press, 1988), 89.

37. Primo Levi, *The Drowned and the Saved* (New York: Vintage, 1988), 12. For a critical analysis of claims about the incomprehensibility and the uniqueness of the Holocaust, see Alan Rosenberg, "The Crisis in Knowing and Understanding the Holocaust," in *Echoes from the Holocaust*, ed. by Alan Rosenberg and Gerald Myers (Philadelphia: Temple University Press, 1988). Rosenberg asks, "Does such hyperbole serve its purpose?" (387) Without a rhetorical treatment of responses to ultimate evil, Rosenberg risks reducing the laments and exasperations of holocaust survivors to "mere exaggeration."

38. Blaise Pascal, *Pensées*, trans. A. J. Krailsheimer (New York: Penguin, 1966), p. 220. It is interesting that in the frontpiece to *Sickness unto Death*, ed. and trans. Howard V. and Edna H. Hong (Princeton University Press, 1980), Kierkegaard reverses Pascal's aphorism: "Lord, give us weak eyes for things of little worth, and eyes clear-sighted in all of your truth."

39. Paul Ramsey connects hope to excess. "Ordinary teachers of wisdom, such as Aristotle, treat hope as an emotion which needs curbing, so that we habituate ourselves to expect only a little—the little we prudently have a right to expect. Christian ethics finds that love for neighbor, measured by the controlling love of Christ, stretches hope far beyond prudent moderation. Christian love goes to the extreme of hoping all things, and this only an everlasting love, or a love perpetually renewed, can accomplish." *Basic Christian Ethics*, 231.

40. Friedrich Nietzsche, *The Will to Power*, trans. Walter Kaufmann and R. J. Hollingdale (New York: Random House, 1967), 396.

41. It is interesting that precisely this transition from an ultimate affirmation of divine love to the command to love one's neighbor was at the crux of Freud's critique of Christian ethics. For Freud, such love, in practice, is unrealistic; it is too disproportionate to both the erotic and the aggressive drives of the most unconscious aspects of the ego. "The commandment [to love one's neighbor as oneself] is impossible to fulfil; such an enormous inflation of love can only lower its value, not get rid of the difficulty." Moreover, "What is the point of a precept enunciated with so much solemnity if its fulfilment cannot be recommended as reasonable?" From *Civilization and Its Discontents*, trans. James Strachey (New York: Norton, 1961), 90 and 57. Freud's scientific realism precisely, even if inadvertently, locates the power of the Christian discourse on love, but it is also a challenge to the theologian to show how such hyperbole makes a difference in life. Interestingly, Nietzsche too found the Christian concept of love to be supremely unrealistic: "Love is the state in which man sees things most decidedly as they are not." From *The Antichrist*, in *The Portable Nietzsche*, ed. Walter Kaufmann (New York: Penguin, 1976), 591.

42. Marvick is saying, it seems to me, to borrow an old phrase, that while all good figures borrow, hyperboles steal. Or, to continue this thought, the white lies of metaphors become blackened by hyperbole. One should note the obvious here: some hyperboles have passed into language as commonplaces, like "I'm freezing to death," "I'd rather die..." or even, "I'd never...," but the same holds true for all of the tropes, especially metaphor.

43. Note, in this context, the use of the term "mannerism" to denote certain paintings that distort and disfigure—exaggerate—the human form; such paintings were often thought to be unnatural, and were only regarded with respect after the First World War, when the Expressionists themselves increasingly relied on exaggeration. Compare, for an example of mannerism, El Greco's "The Opening of

Notes 173

the Fifth Seal" to any of Dürer's careful engravings, or note the history of the reception of Grünewald's masterpieces, and our lack of knowledge about that painter (it is unlikely that Grünewald, for example, was the painter's name). Although such paintings are "mannered," their stylistic configurations are hardly obvious and their power is impossible to deny. The connection between hyperbole and the mannered, distorted style will be important for my analysis of Flannery O'Connor in chapter 5.

Chapter 2.

1. David Tracy, *Plurality and Ambiguity*, 97.

2. For this label see Richard Swinburne, *Responsibility and Atonement* (Oxford: Clarendon Press, 1989). "A total morality, by contrast [to limited moralities], tells one what to do in all circumstances. It asks for everything—though it may offer a choice of ways of fulfillment" (19).

3. Gene Outka, *Agape, An Ethical Analysis* (New Haven: Yale University Press, 1972). The only full length treatment of *Works of Love* in English is Gene Fendt, *Works of Love?: Reflections on Works of Love* (Potomac, Md.: Scripta Humanistica, n.d.). Fendt, reacting against Paul Müller's conservative Danish commentary, reads Kierkegaard's book as a secret message to Regina, a poststructuralist communication of seduction and intrigue, not theology and ethics. He admits that his reading is a (barely) possible interpretation with little or no evidence (see 18–19). For an excellent reading of *Works of Love* that situates Kierkegaard's thought in the social and economic history of Denmark, drawing out its political connections and implications, see Bruce H. Kirmmse, *Kierkegaard in Golden Age Denmark* (Bloomington: Indiana University Press, 1990), chapter 19.

4. See for example Judith Plaskow's groundbreaking work, *Sex, Sin and Grace* (Lanham: University Press of America, 1980).

5. Theodor W. Adorno, "On Kierkegaard's Doctrine of Love," in *Søren Kierkegaard*, ed. Harold Bloom (New York: Chelsea House Publishers, 1989). Originally published in *Studies in Philosophy and Social Science* 8 (1939). For the fullest statement of Adorno's critique of Kierkegaard, see his first published philosophical work, *Kierkegaard, Construction of the Aesthetic*, trans. Robert Hullot-Kentor (Minneapolis: University of Minnesota Press, 1989).

6. It is fascinating that in this book, which is an impressionis-

tic work overflowing with bold assertions and fantastic causal leaps, Adorno and Horkheimer recognize as the configurative power of their prose the same trope that governs Kierkegaard's discourse: "But only exaggeration is true." *Dialectic of Enlightenment* (New York: Continuum, 1972), 118.

7. See for example Louis Mackey's two books, *Kierkegaard: A Kind of Poet* (Philadelphia: University of Pennsylvania Press, 1971) and *Points of View: Readings of Kierkegaard* (Tallahassee: Florida State University Press, 1986).

8. Theodor W. Adorno, *Minima Moralia*, trans. E. F. N. Jephcott (London: Verso, 1978), 126–7. For other comments on hyperbole in this text, see pp. 80 and 86. For secondary literature about the role of hyperbole in Adorno's thought, see Martin Jay, *Adorno* (Cambridge: Harvard, 1984), 15, 60, and 102; and Gillian Rose, *The Melancholy Science* (New York: Columbia, 1978), 5 and 20.

9. Søren Kierkegaard, *Fear and Trembling/Repetition*, ed. and trans. Howard V. Hong and Edna H. Hong (Princeton: Princeton University Press, 1983), 133.

10. *Minima Moralia*, 86.

11. Søren Kierkegaard, *Training in Christianity*, trans. Walter Lowrie (Princeton: Princeton University Press, 1967), 55.

12. Søren Kierkegaard, *The Sickness unto Death*, ed. and trans. Howard V. Hong and Edna Hong (Princeton University Press, 1980), 22.

13. Søren Kierkegaard, *Purity of Heart is to Will One Thing*, trans. Douglas V. Steere (New York: Harper and Row, 1938), 61.

14. Søren Kierkegaard, *The Point of View for My Work as an Author: A Report to History*, trans. and intro. Walter Lowrie (New York: Harper and Brothers, 1962).

15. Walter Lowrie, *Kierkegaard*, vol. 2 (New York: Harper and Brothers, 1962), 490.

16. Søren Kierkegaard, *Works of Love*, trans. Howard and Edna Hong (New York: Harper and Row, 1962).

17. Quoted in translators' introduction to *Works of Love*, 12.

18. Ibid., 18.

19. For a good introduction to Bataille's thought, especially his connections among expenditure, sacrifice, sex, and death, see *Erotism, Death and Sensuality*, trans. Mary Dalwood (San Francisco:

City Lights Books, 1986). I will return to a fuller analysis of Bataille in chapter 3.

20. Shakespeare catches the exhaustion and ennui to which excess can too easily lead in the opening lines of *Twelfth Night*: "If music be the food of love, play on, give me excess of it; that surfeiting, the appetite may sicken, and so die."

21. Emmanuel Levinas, *Totality and Infinity*, trans. Alphonso Lingis (Pittsburgh: Duquesne University Press, 1969). Note the following representative comment: "The being that presents himself in the face comes from a dimension of height, a dimension of transcendence whereby he can present himself as a stranger without opposing me as obstacle or enemy" (213). Jacques Derrida has commented on the hyperbole of the infinitely high other, "the superlative excess, the spatial literality of the metaphor. No matter how high it is, height is always accessible; the most high, however, is higher than height. No addition of more height will ever measure it. It does not belong to space, is not of this world." From "Violence and Metaphysics," in *Writing and Difference*, trans. Alan Bass (Chicago: University of Chicago Press, 1978), 93. Martin Buber, who influenced much of Levinas's work, can also be discussed in terms of hyperbole. Note the way in which Walter Kaufmann, in the prologue to *I and Thou* (New York: Charles Scribner's Sons, 1970), resists the superlative style of this book. "Certainly Buber's delight in language gets between him and his readers" (19). "Even more than Nietzsche's *Zarathustra*, it is overwritten" (23). "It represents a late flowering of romanticism and tends to blur all contours in the twilight of suggestive but extremely unclear language" (24). "The style seems mannered" (25). "Buber's most significant ideas are not tied to his extraordinary language" (25). These painfully obvious attempts to resist the rhetorical power of this text do not do justice to its own self-conscious configurations; the parallels with readings of Kierkegaard's *Works of Love* are unnerving. Note one passage from Buber's text in which he practically defines the I-You relationship in terms of hyperbole: "Their [the You-moments] spell may be seductive, but they pull us dangerously to extremes, loosening the well-tried structure, leaving behind more doubt than satisfaction, shaking up our security—altogether uncanny, altogether indispensable" (84–5).

22. This is not to deny the many connections between Levinas's philosophy and his biblical and theological ideas and discussions. For his own analysis of these interrelations, see his conversations with Phillipe Nemo, *Ethics and Infinity*, trans. Richard A. Cohen (Pittsburgh: Duquesne University Press, 1985). By inferring ethics from a phenomenology of consciousness, Levinas comes

close to subsuming the problem of the other under the problem of perception and thus defusing the power and strangeness of his claims.

Chapter 3.

1. Georges Bataille's (1897–1962) position in French culture is profound but ambiguous, so it is no surprise that his influence in the English-speaking world is late to develop. Many of his books have been translated only recently, and he is known more for his erotic fiction than his theory of religion. For one of the few theological reflections on Bataille, see Mark C. Taylor, *Tears* (Albany: State University of New York Press, 1990). Taylor, conflating Bataille and Derrida, writes about an excess that is powerful yet unsayable: "In an effort to avoid madness, the philosopher struggles to erase surplus and excess by repressing the Holy in and through the reduction of difference to identity, and Other to same" (107). Excess is totally other and thus merely different. For Taylor on the connection between Bataille and sacrifice, see "The Politics of Theo-ry," *Journal of the American Academy of Religion* (Spring 1991): 1–37. Also see chapter 5 of Taylor's *Altarity* (Chicago: University of Chicago Press, 1987).

2. Bataille's work develops Nietzsche's portrait of the Dionysian element of life with an accent on the liberating effects of confronting suffering from strength, without resentment or excuse. As Nietzsche writes in *Twilight of the Gods*, trans. R. J. Hollingdale (New York: Penguin, 1990): "Affirmation of life even in its strangest and sternest problems, the will to life rejoicing in its own inexhaustibility through the *sacrifice* of its highest types—*that* is what I call Dionysian, *that* is what I recognized as the bridge to the psychology of the *tragic* poet. *Not* so as to get rid of pity and terror, not so as to purify oneself of a dangerous emotion through its vehement discharge—it was thus Aristotle understood it—: but, beyond pity and terror, *to realize in oneself* the eternal joy of becoming—that joy which also encompasses *joy in destruction*..." (120). In the same work Nietzsche offers a fascinating definition of strength: "Only excess of strength is proof of strength" (31). In contrast to Nietzsche, however, Bataille is not very hopeful about the Dionysian quest; he finds in excess an incompletion and a fragmentation that belie some of Nietzsche's more exuberant and optimistic passages. Moreover, Bataille frames excess in an oddly pious religious language that Nietzsche too sometimes spoke but could not acknowledge.

3. Note Nietzsche on luxury: "*Luxury.*—An inclination for luxury extends into the depths of a man: it betrays the fact that superfluity and immoderation is the water in which his soul most likes to swim." *Daybreak*, trans. R. J. Hollingdale (Cambridge: University of Cambridge Press, 1982), 413 (number 405). The tone of this aphorism is not clear. Nietzsche often praises self-denial and renunciation as the necessary prerequisites for healthy exercises of the will to power, but he also celebrated a joyful laughter and a Dionysian dance that would go beyond the all-too-reasonable confines of traditional morality. Bataille combines these two routes by arguing that self-sacrifice is excess. The place of excess in Nietzsche's work is ambiguous. For his defense of moderation against excess, see the very anti-Bataille observation in section 38 of *Human, All Too Human*, trans. by Marion Faber, with Stephen Lehmann (Lincoln: University of Nebraska Press, 1984), 42–43.

4. For a similar but more positive evaluation of the capacity of the festival or the carnival to provide a forceful expression of the rebellion against official, high culture and its sanctioning institutions, see Mikhail Bakhtin, *Rabelais and His World*, trans. Helene Iswolsky (Bloomington: Indiana University Press, 1984). Also note Victor Turner's analysis of rites of passage as liminal or transitional phases where the neophyte literally stands nowhere, in a sacred nonspace, outside of society in order to become more fully integrated into the group. Turner uses the analysis of exaggeration and distortion to explain some features of this experience in primordial traditions. See *The Forest of Symbols* (Ithaca: Cornell University Press, 1967), chapter 4. Of related interest is Freud's comment that "excess is of the essence of a festival," in *Totem and Taboo*, trans. James Strachey (New York: W. W. Norton, 1950), 174.

5. For translations of his fiction, see *Story of the Eye*, trans. Joachim Neugroschal (New York: Penguin, 1982); *L'Abbé C*, trans. Philip A. Facey (New York: Marion Boyars, 1988); *Blue of Noon*, trans. Harry Mathews (New York: Marion Boyars, 1986); *My Mother, Madame Edwarda, The Dead Man*, trans. Austryn Wainhouse (New York: Marion Boyars, 1989). For some selections from Bataille's fiction and several appreciative essays see Paul Buck, ed., *Violent Silence, Celebrating Georges Bataille* (The Georges Bataille Event, 1984). For Bataille's literary criticism, see *Literature and Evil*, trans. Alastair Hamilton (New York: Marion Boyars, 1985).

6. Jacques Derrida, "From Restricted to General Economy: A Hegelianism without Reserve," *Writing and Difference*, trans. Alan Bass (Chicago: University of Chicago Press, 1978), 252–53.

7. Quotations from *Inner Experience*, trans. and intro. Leslie

Anne Boldt (Albany: SUNY Press, 1988) and *Guilty*, trans. Bruce Boone and intro. Denis Hollier (Venice, Calif.: Lapis Press, 1988) will be cited in the text according to the abreviations *IE* and *G*.

8. Note, for example, the following: "By definition, the extreme limit of the 'possible' is that point where, despite the unintelligible position which it has for him in being, man, having stripped himself of enticement and fear, advances so far that one cannot conceive of the possibility of going further" (*IE*, 39).

9. Nietzsche, in fact, substituted a notion of expenditure for sacrifice. He thought that sacrifice was born of weakness and resentment, whereas strength produces extravagant acts that overflow from the healthy will. "Why sacrifice? I squander [*verschwende*] what is given me, I—a squanderer with a thousand hands; how could I call that sacrificing?" *Thus Spoke Zarathustra*, trans. Walter Kaufmann (New York: Penguin Books, 1966), 238. Instead of opposing sacrifice and excess, Bataille identifies them.

10. A significant passage is worth quoting in full: "The privileged manifestation of Negativity is death, but death, in fact, reveals nothing. In theory, it is his natural, animal being whose death reveals Man to himself, but the revelation never takes place. For when the animal being supporting him dies, the human being himself ceases to be. In order for Man to reveal himself ultimately to himself, he would have to die, but he would have to do it while living—watching himself ceasing to be. In other words, death itself would have to become (self-)consciousness at the very moment that it annihilates the conscious being. In a sense, this is what takes place (what at least is on the point of taking place, or which takes place in a fugitive, ungraspable manner) by means of a subterfuge. In the sacrifice, the sacrificer identifies himself with the animal that is struck down dead. And so he dies in seeing himself die, and even, in a certain way, by his own will, one in spirit with the sacrifical weapon. But it is a comedy!" From "Hegel, Death and Sacrifice," trans. Jonathan Strauss, in *On Bataille, Yale French Studies* 78 (1990): 19. There is little evidence that sacrificers in primordial cultures identified themselves with the sacrificed animal. Bataille's point, however, exceeds a theory of primitive sacrifice: only this particular religious ritual does justice to the negative moment of death that lies at the center of life, but even this ritual cannot capture that which pushes life beyond itself. Much of Bataille's fiction is an attempt to depict acts of sacrifice that lead to demonic laughter—in full awareness of this dilemma—rather than to self-righteous somberness.

11. One could argue that here Bataille is being true to the Nietzschean corpus; although Nietzsche rants and raves against the

ethic of sacrifice, Christian love, he himself finds a kind of redemption, or at least self-affirmation, in acts of destruction. The new, true, and good can only arise from the collapse of the old, from violently going beyond tradition, custom, and religion.

12. The unreliabilty of language is a major theme of both *Inner Experience* and *Guilty*. In a fragment included as an appendix to *Guilty*, Bataille connects the trust in language as representation or idealization with Christianity: "Basically Christianity is only a crystallization of language. The solemn assertion of the fourth Gospel—*Et verbum caro factum est*—is in a sense this deep truth: the truth of language is Christian. If you assume man and language as doubling the real world with another world, imagined and available when evoked—then Christianity is necessary. Or if not, then some analogous assertion" (134).

13. *Erotism, Death and Sensuality*, trans. Mary Dalwood (San Francisco: City Lights, 1986). Cited in the text as *E*.

14. For Freud's honest confession of his own inability to understand mystical experience, due to his fear of the loss of the autonomous self, see the opening pages of *Civilization and Its Discontents*, trans. James Strachey (New York: W. W. Norton, 1961). What Freud denies Bataille embraces, but both interpret mysticism as a regressive loss of self-identity.

15. For a brief but insightful reading of Bataille in terms of the dynamic of domination and submission, see Jessica Benjamin, *The Bonds of Love* (New York: Pantheon Books, 1988), 62–68. Benjamin criticizes Bataille's views from the viewpoint of a feminist theory of eroticism that allows for acts of mutual recognition and intersubjective give and take.

16. Michel Foucault, "A Preface to Transgression," *Language, Counter-Memory, Practice*, ed. Donald F. Bouchard (Ithaca: Cornell University Press, 1977), 34.

17. Ibid., 35.

18. Much of Bataille's argument against Christianity pivots on a reading of the Christianization of the Roman Empire and Europe as a usurpation and extermination of paganism. Many scholars have begun to note the continuities between pagan religious practices and Christianity, not just the discontinuities. For one excellent study that focuses on the rise of asceticism as the criterion of Christian commitment (an asceticism that had, it should be noted, roots in Greek philosophy and, in its Christian form, was increasingly connected to the search for perfect communal living), see Robert

Markus, *The End of Ancient Christianity* (Cambridge: Cambridge University Press, 1990). As I noted in chapter 1, the pagan world too had its difficulties with excess. All religions both promote and organize (that is, restrict) excess. I agree with Bataille that the danger of Christianity is its tendency to moralize and spiritualize excess; its strength is that it tries to direct excess toward the other. In any case, a strong dichotomy between paganism and Christianity cannot withstand the historical evidence.

19. For Bataille, temptation is basic to the expression of freedom: "Temptation is the desire to fall, to fail, to faint and to squander all one's reserves until there is no firm ground beneath one's feet" (*E*, 240).

20. Michele H. Richman, *Reading Georges Bataille, Beyond the Gift* (Baltimore: The Johns Hopkins University Press, 1982), 52.

21. Denis Hollier, *Against Architecture: The Writings of Georges Bataille*, trans. Betsy Wing (Cambridge: MIT Press, 1989), 103.

22. Denis Hollier, ed. and intro., *The College of Sociology, 1937–39*, trans. Betsy Wing (Minneapolis: University of Minnesota Press, 1988), xix. "Heterology is not a product of the aestheticization of the repugnant. Disgust here is not a modality of aesthetic experience but a fundamental existential dimension. Reactions of repulsion do not have to be induced: they are what is given to start with" (xix). Jürgen Habermas finds this paradox intolerable: Bataille's theory reaches beyond reason to thematize that which destroys reason. "At this point, however, the knowing subject would—paradoxically—have to surrender his own identity and yet retrieve those experiences to which he was exposed in ecstasy—to catch them like fish from the decentered ocean of emotions." *The Philosophical Discourse of Modernity*, trans. Frederick G. Lawrence (Cambridge: MIT Press, 1987), 236.

23. Georges Bataille, *Visions of Excess, Selected Writings, 1927–1939*, ed. Allan Stoekl and trans. Allan Stoekl with Carl R. Lovitt and Donald M. Leslie, Jr. (Minneapolis: University of Minnesota Press, 1985). This book will be cited as *VE*.

24. In the letter to Kojève, Bataille writes: "Religion makes negativity an object of contemplation better than a tragedy or a painting. But negativity isn't recognized *as such* in the artwork or in the emotional elements of religion. Just the opposite: it's introduced into a system that nullifies it, and only the affirmation is recognized" (*G*, 124). Bataille was tremendously influenced by Kojève's lectures on Hegel. See *Introduction to the Reading of Hegel*, ed. Allan

Bloom and trans. James H. Nichols, Jr. (Ithaca: Cornell University Press, 1980). However, against Kojève's notion of the end of history—the synthesis of the master and slave dialectic in the communist workers' state—Bataille opposes an excessive desire that is essentially a-historical, incapable of sublation or resolution in social organizations. As Derrida explains, "The necessity of logical continuity is the decision or interpretive milieu of all Hegelian interpretations. In interpreting negativity as labor, in betting for discourse, meaning, history, etc. Hegel has bet against play, against chance." "From Restricted to General Economy," 260. There is some question, however, whether Bataille's pursuit of negativity *as such*, excess in itself, does not ironically lead him to a similar impasse between explanation or representation and negation or excess.

25. Marcel Mauss, *The Gift*, trans. Ian Cunnison (New York: Norton, 1967, originally published 1925). Mauss (1872–1950) was Durkheim's nephew and principal intellectual heir.

26. Some of Mauss's critique of modern giving—prompted by pity and not an expression of strength—echoes Nietzsche: "Charity wounds him who receives, and our whole moral effort is directed towards suppressing the unconscious harmful patronage of the rich almoner" (63). Overall, Mauss is optimistic about the return of the gift: "Today the ancient principles are making their influence felt upon the rigours, abstractions and inhumanities of our codes. From this point of view much of our law is in process of reformulation and some of our innovations consist in putting back the clock" (64).

27. *The Accursed Share, An Essay on General Economics*, vol. 1, trans. Robert Hurley (New York: Zone Books, 1988). This book will be cited in the text as *AS*.

28. Habermas, *The Philosophical Discourse of Modernity*, 235.

29. *Theory of Religion*, trans. Robert Hurley (New York: Zone Books, 1989). Cited in the text as *TR*.

30. When Bataille writes about the Protestant Reformation, he always means not Luther but Calvin, and not really Calvin but Calvinism as interpreted by Max Weber.

31. In *The Way of Jesus Christ, Christology in Messianic Dimensions*, trans. Margaret Kohl (San Francisco: Harper, 1990), Jürgen Moltmann emphasizes the excessive nature of the Christian remembrance of the hope in resurrection. Resurrection cannot be reduced to crucifixion: "Christ's resurrection has an added value and a surplus of promise over Christ's death...This surplus of Christ's resurrection over his death is manifested in the surplus of grace

compared with the mere cancellation of sin" (186). Moreover: "In the historical religions, the precedence of the horizon of expectation over the sphere of historical experience is based on the surplus of promise, which exceeds the historical fulfillments of promise. This surplus for its part is founded on the inexhaustibility of the creative God, who 'arrives at his rest' only when heaven and earth are in complete correspondence with him" (238). I will return to the question of Jesus Christ in the last chapter.

32. Bataille also articulates a longing for hope in *Lascaux, Or the Birth of Art*, trans. Austryn Wainhouse (Paris: Skira, 1955): "We often belittle, call childish this need to be wonderstruck...but we set right off again in search of the wonderful. That which we hold worthy of our love is always that which overwhelms us: it is the unhoped-for, the thing that is beyond hoping for" (15).

33. It is fascinating that after the passage from Durkheim that serves as the opening quotation of this chapter, Durkheim qualifies his emphasis on the extravagance of religious acts and returns to a more functionalist approach with a warning against hyperbole: "One would certainly commit the gravest error if he saw only this one aspect of religion, or if he even exaggerated its importance. When a rite serves only to distract, it is no longer a rite. The moral forces expressed by religious symbols are real forces with which we must reckon and with which we cannot do what we will." *The Elementary Forms of the Religious Life*, trans. Joseph Ward Swain (New York: The Free Press, 1965), 427. Durkheim tries to do justice to both the disruptive and radical exuberance of religious acts and their moral and social seriousness. Bataille is not interested in restricting hyperbole at all, while I am trying to show that hyperbole, pushed to its very limits, insinuates sense.

Chapter 4.

1. The classic statement of this position is from O'Connor's close friend, John Hawkes, "Flannery O'Connor's Devil," *Sewanee Review* 70 (1962): 395–407. This intentional and creative misreading has sparked many imitations. Brainard Cheney called it "a *tour de force* remarkable only for foolhardiness," in his "Miss O'Connor Creates Unusual Humor Out of Ordinary Sin," *Sewanee Review* 71 (1963): 646. For works that are generally situated in this tradition, see Robert H. Brinkmeyer, Jr., *The Art and Vision of Flannery O'Connor* (Baton Rouge: Louisiana State University Press, 1981); Edward Kessler, *Flannery O'Connor and the Language of Apocalypse* (Princeton University Press, 1986); and Frederick Asals, "The Limits of

Explanation," *Critical Essays on Flannery O'Connor*, ed. Melvin J. Friedman and Beverly Lyon Clark (Boston: G.K. Hall, 1985). Note the interesting comment by Josephine Hendin in *World of Flannery O'Connor* (Bloomington: Indiana University Press, 1970): "If she set out to make morals, to praise the old values, she ended by engulfing all of them in icy violence. If she began by mocking or damning her murderous heroes, she ended by exalting them. She grew to celebrate the liberating power of destruction. O'Connor became more and more the pure poet of the Misfit, the oppressed, the psychic cripple, the freak—all of those who are martyred by silent fury and redeemed through violence" (42).

2. See, for example, many of the essays in Melvin J. Friedman and Lewis A. Lawson, eds., *The Added Dimension, The Art and Mind of Flannery O'Connor* (New York: Fordham University Press, 1966); David Eggenschwiler, *The Christian Humanism of Flannery O'Connor* (Detroit: Wayne State University Press, 1972); Carter W. Martin, *The True Country, Themes in the Fiction of Flannery O'Connor* (Nashville: Vanderbilt University Press, 1969); Thomas M. Carlson, "Flannery O'Connor: The Manichaean Dilemma," *Sewanee Review* 77 (1969): 254–76; Ralph C. Wood, *The Comedy of Redemption* (University of Notre Dame Press, 1988); and the interesting homage to O'Connor by Marion Montgomery, *Why Flannery O'Connor Stayed Home* (LaSalle Ill.: Sherwood Sugden, 1981).

3. As a sign of the ambiguity, note Harold Bloom's gnostic reading of O'Connor in his introduction to the excellent collection of essays in *Flannery O'Connor* (New York: Chelsea House, 1986) where he acknowledges but deplores the theological overtones in her work: "Her pious admirers to the contrary, O'Connor would have bequeathed us even stronger novels and stories, of the eminence of Faulkner's, if she had been able to restrain her spiritual tendentiousness" (8).

4. I will try to give an original reading of hyperbole in O'Connor, so I will not overburden the reader with references to the incredible number of secondary studies. For a typical comment, note the following: "Through willful exaggeration of both plot and character, O'Connor seeks to demonstrate the disfiguring effects of evil." Wood, *The Comedy of Redemption*, 97. Comments like this are rarely followed by any specific rhetorical analysis of hyperbole.

5. Geoffrey Galt Harpham, *On the Grotesque, Strategies of Contradiction in Art and Literature*, (Princeton University Press, 1982), 3. For his own reading of O'Connor, see 185–89. For a theological reading of the grotesque in O'Connor, see Preston Mercer Browning, Jr., *Flannery O'Connor and the Grotesque Recovery of the*

Holy (Ph.D. diss., University of Chicago Divinity School, 1969). Browning argues that O'Connor reclaims the holy only by a journey through the radically profane, and he connects the grotesque to exaggeration (see 27). For a historical overview of the grotesque, see Wolfgang Kayser, *The Grotesque in Art and Literature*, trans. Ulrich Weisstein (Bloomington: Indiana University Press, 1963). He defines the grotesque as the estranged world (184) and, more specifically, "an attempt to invoke and subdue the demonic aspects of the world" (188).

6. Harpham actually connects the grotesque with myth: "The grotesque consists of the manifest, visible, or unmediated presence of mythic or primitive elements *in* a nonmythic or modern context" (51). Certainly the juxtaposition of myth and secularity can be upsetting and surprising, but in my reading the grotesque is an extension of the ordinary that leads to the unreal only by showing how far the real can be stretched almost but not quite beyond recognition.

7. Flannery O'Connor, *Mystery and Manners*, ed. Sally and Robert Fitzgerald (New York: Farrar, Straus and Giroux, 1961), 33. Hereafter cited in the text as *MM*. Also note this comment: "The sharper the light of faith, the more glaring are apt to be the distortions the writer sees in the life around him" (26).

8. See Gilbert H. Muller, *Nightmares and Visions, Flannery O'Connor and the Catholic Grotesque* (Athens: University of Georgia Press, 1972). For a religious analysis of the gothic, see Rudolf Otto, *The Idea of the Holy*, trans. John Harvey (New York: Oxford, 1978), 67–68. Many of O'Connor's stories seem to depict the mood that Otto describes as the *mysterium tremendum*, the simultaneously fascinating and terrifying experience of the nonrational numinous. There are significant differences, though. Whereas the uncanny feeling of awe that Otto describes is basically one of reverence and rapture, O'Connor, in contrast, does not push her fiction toward mysticism. She tries to portray the disorienting disruption of the apparent continuity of experience, the moment when the world collapses and the self is unbearably exposed, stripped of all support and shelter.

9. "Melodrama is above all a democratic genre of popular art, designed for large mass audiences ignorant of artistic tradition and indiscriminating in matters of culture, but avid for robust entertainment and rudimentary moral instruction." Daniel C. Gerould, "The Americanization of Melodrama," in *American Melodrama* (New York: Performing Arts Journal Publications, 1983), 8.

10. Peter Brooks, *The Melodramatic Imagination, Balzac, Henry James, and the Mode of Excess* (New Haven: Yale University Press, 1976), ix.

11. Ibid., 41. Also note this comment from Brooks: "Things cease to be merely themselves, gestures cease to be merely tokens of social intercourse whose meaning is assigned by a social code; they become the vehicles of metaphors whose tenor suggests another kind of reality" (9).

12. Ibid., 41. At one point in his book, Brooks also offers a linguistic definition: "This is the mode of excess: The postulation of a signified in excess of the possibilities of the signifier, which in turn produces an excessive signifier, making large but unsubstantial claims on meaning" (199).

13. O'Connor worried about subtlety: "I am not one of the subtle sensitive writers like Eudora Welty. I see only what is outside and what sticks out a mile, such things as the sun that nobody has to uncover or be bright to see. When I first started to write, I was much worried over not being subtle but it don't worry me any more" (141). She also hyperbolically denounced it: "Subtlety is the curse of man. It is not found in the deity" (452). Both quotes are from O'Connor's collected letters in Sally Fitzgerald, ed., *The Habit of Being* (New York: Farrar, Straus, and Girous, 1988), hereafter cited as *HB*.

14. "One old lady who wants her heart lifted up wouldn't be so bad, but you multiply her two hundred and fifty thousand times and what you get is a book club" (*MM*, 48).

15. "This story ['A Good Man is Hard to Find'] has been called grotesque, but I prefer to call it literal. A good story is literal in the same sense that a child's drawing is literal. When a child draws, he doesn't intend to distort but to set down exactly what he sees, and as his gaze is direct, he sees the lines that create motion. Now the lines of motion that interest the writer are usually the invisible. They are lines of spiritual motion" (*MM*, 113). And note this comment: "The prophet is a realist of distances, and it is this kind of realism that goes into great novels. It is the realism which does not hesitate to distort appearances in order to show a hidden truth" (*MM*, 179).

16. Notice this comment in Robert Fitzgerald's introduction to *Everything That Rises Must Converge* (New York: Farrar, Straus, and Giroux, 1965), hereafter cited in the text as *ETR*: "For one thing, it is evident that the writer deliberately and indeed indifferently, almost defiantly, restricted her horizontal range: a pasture scene and a fortress wall of pine woods reappear like a signature in story after

story. The same is true of her social range and range of idiom. But these restrictions, like the very humility of her style, are all deceptive. The true range of the stories is vertical and Dantesque in what is taken in, in scale of implication" (xxii).

17. "Of course I hear the complaint over and over that there is no sense in writing about people who disgust you. I think there is; but the fact is that the people I write about certainly don't disgust me entirely though I see them from a standard of judgment from which they fall short" (*HB*, 221). "I'm a Catholic but this [the Incarnation] is in orthodox Protestantism also, though out of context—which makes it grow into grotesque forms. The Catholic, using his own eyes and the eyes of the Church (when he is inclined to open them) is in a most favorable position to recognize the grotesque" (*HB*, 227). Also note this fascinating admission: "I know nothing harder than making good people believable" (*HB*, 129).

18. "Distortion in this case is an instrument; exaggeration has a purpose and the whole structure of the story or novel has been made what it is because of belief. This is not the kind of distortion that destroys; it is the kind that reveals, or should reveal" (*MM*, 162).

19. "I am interested in making up a good case for distortion as I am coming to believe it is the only way to make people see" (*HB*, 79).

20. "I don't know if anybody can be converted without seeing themselves in a kind of blasting annihilating light, a blast that will last a lifetime" (*HB*, 427).

21. O'Connor understood the pain of grace: "This notion that grace is healing omits the fact that before it heals it cuts with the sword Christ said he came to bring" (*HB*, 411).

22. "Often the nature of grace can be made plain only by describing its absence" (*MM*, 204). "It may be a matter of recognizing the Holy Ghost in fiction by the way He chooses to conceal himself" (*HB*, 130).

23. Frederick Asals, *Flannery O'Connor, The Language of Extremity* (Athens: University of Georgia Press, 1982), 2. "The litotes of the plain style and the hyperbole of gesture and action, the containment implied by the craft and control and the unleashing dramatized in the rampant feelings and violent plots, the manners of the local, the everyday, the ordinary and the mystery of the devastating intrusions of psychic and cosmic forces, the laughter induced by the comic and the terror evoked by violence—out of all these dualities comes the vibrant tension that gives her work its disturbing power" (131).

24. Ibid., 3.

25. The devil "is not simply generalized evil, but an evil intelligence determined on its own supremacy" (*MM*, 168). "I want to be certain that the Devil gets identified as the Devil and not simply taken for this or that psychological tendency" (*HB*, 360). "Anyway, it occurs to me to put forward that fiction writing is not an exercise in clarity, except of course as one is expected to give the devil his due—something I have at least been scrupulous about" (*HB*, 103).

26. Note her interesting confession about "The Lame Shall Enter First": "In this one, I'll admit that the Devil's voice is my own" (*HB*, 464). She also explains her preference for miring her stories in evil with this statement: "In the gospels it was the devils who first recognized Christ and the evangelists didn't censor this information" (*HB*, 517).

27. "Experience is the greatest deterrent to fiction" (*HB*, 284).

28. "The religion of the South is a do-it-yourself religion, something which I as a Catholic find painful and touching and grimly comic. It's full of unconscious pride that lands them in all sorts of ridiculous religious predicaments. They have nothing to correct their practical heresies and so they work them out dramatically. If this were merely comic to me, it would be no good, but I accept the same fundamental doctrines of sin and redemption and judgment that they do" (*HB*, 350). "One of the good things about Protestantism is that it always contains the seeds of its own reversal. It is open at both ends—at one end to Catholicism, at the other to unbelief" (*HB*, 411). Roman Catholic fanatics join the monasteries, while Protestant fanatics "go about in the world getting into all sorts of trouble and drawing the wrath of people who don't believe in anything much at all down on your head" (*HB*, 517).

29. Indeed, her theological beliefs, in almost humorous contrast to her prose, are always casually understated: "The truth in any such matter as this [religion] is always a great deal more stodgy-sounding than what we would like to believe" (*HB*, 147).

30. "One of the effects of modern liberal Protestantism has been gradually to turn religion into poetry and therapy, to make truth vaguer and vaguer and more and more relative, to banish intellectual distinctions, to depend on feeling instead of thought, and gradually to come to believe that God has no power, that he cannot communicate with us, cannot reveal himself to us, indeed has not done so, and that religion is our own sweet invention" (*HB*, 479). "I am only really interested in a fiction of miracles" (*HB*, 413–4).

31. Carol Shloss, "Epiphany," in Bloom, ed., *Flannery O'Connor*, 80. She also argues that "to 'shout' in fiction about any belief, Christian or otherwise, is done effectively, not by leaving norms or opinions implicit in the text, reachable if at all through inference, but by interpreting events explicitly, through the privileges of the omnisciently narrated tale, or by making man's encounter with religion the explicit topic of discussion" (66).

32. See Dietrich Bonhoeffer, *Letters and Papers from Prison*, ed. Eberhard Bethge (New York: Macmillan, 1972), 279–82.

33. It is often said that irony turns appearances against itself while hyperbole, somewhat superficially and trustworthily, extends appearances as far as they will go. Irony negates, while hyperbole multiplies. Perhaps O'Connor can teach us that hyperbole too has a negative power, pushing the known to the point where it becomes not unknown but troubling and disturbing, an unwanted known that displays all previous knowns as deficient and incomplete. I will return to this comparison of irony and hyperbole in chapter 6.

Chapter 5.

1. Paul West, "In Defense of Purple Prose," *New York Times Book Review*, Dec. 15, 1985, p. 1.

2. In one of Nietzsche's most gentle and least hyperbolic books, he aphoristically defines inflated prose in a way that, ironically, can easily apply to his own later work (think, for example, of *Ecce Homo*): "*The inflated style.*—An artist who wants, not to discharge his high-swollen feelings in his work and so unburden himself, but rather to communicate precisely this feeling of swollenness, is bombastic, and his style is the inflated style." *Daybreak*, trans. R. J. Hollingdale (Cambridge: Cambridge University Press, 1982), 162 (number 332).

3. For a fascinating exploration of the possibilities of a 'jolly' theology, as well as an account of the groundlessness of thought distinct from Derrida's, see Steven Smith, *The Concept of the Spiritual* (Philadelphia: Temple University Press, 1988), 150–55. There is a robust joviality in Chesterton's work that theologians today, overly anxious about method and mournful about the decline of religion and the increasing marginalization of theology in both the church and the academy, could do well to imitate.

4. See the wonderful collection of reviews in D. J. Conlon, *G. K. Chesterton, The Critical Judgments, Part 1: 1900–1937* (Antwerp:

Antwerp Studies in English Literature, 1976). Most of the reviews focus on his perhaps tiresome use of paradox. "Mr. Chesterton is suffering from himself. He early obtained a reputation for paradox, and he seems a little too anxious to live up to the reputation. Now paradoxes are excellent as a flavouring to style, but they are fatal as a foundation, since their effect must rely on their unexpectedness, and used as they are by Mr. Chesterton one expects nothing else" (105). Other reviews focus on his alleged flippancy: "Mr. Chesterton is always like the clown at the fair, who plays tricks before the people to show what a funny fellow he is" (120). Chesterton's good friend Hilaire Belloc wrote one of the best analyses of his style, but it is marred by focusing too singularly on one rhetorical device, what he calls parallelism but what is more commonly called analogy. See *On the Place of Gilbert Chesterton in English Letters* (Shepherdstown, W.V.: Patmos Press, 1977, originally published 1940). "He continually illumined and explained realities by comparisons. This was really the weapon peculiar to Chesterton's genius" (40–41). "Parallelism consists in the illustration of some unperceived truth by its exact consonance with the reflection of a truth already known and perceived" (60). I will argue that the reason for Chesterton's abundantly analogical imagination is a heightened sense of the wonder and beauty of the world that is essentially hyperbolic; his surprising and startling celebration of the joy of life allows him to draw the most unpredictable and uncanny analogies.

5. G. K. Chesterton, *The Autobiography*, from *The Collected Works of G. K. Chesterton*, ed., George J. Marlin, et. al., vol. 16 (San Francisco: St. Ignatius Press, 1988), 163.

6. See the collection of secondary criticism in D. J. Conlon, *G. K. Chesterton, A Half Century of Views* (Oxford: Oxford University Press, 1987). Many writers appreciatively note his extravagant style. H. Marshall McLuhan: "When his exuberant fancy may decorate an argument as a gargoyle embellishes a buttress, the buttress is there; and just as the buttress is there, so is the lofty edifices which it supports...His energetic hatchet-like phrases hew out sharply defined images that are like silhouette or a wood-cut" (8). Herbert Palmer: "G. K. Chesterton, in spite of his frequent blare and bombast, has been extraordinarily successful in infusing true poetry into his thundering orchestra" (15). Dorothy L. Sayers: "Like a beneficent bomb, he blew out of the Church a quantity of stained glass of a very poor period, and let in gusts of fresh air" (123). Ronald Knox: "He never knew his medium, because every medium he tried—and how many he tried!—was too small a receptacle for the amount of himself he put into it" (133). Wilfred Sheed: He had "too much to say and too many ways to say it" (163). Moreover, he was "one of the

loudest, truest voices for sanity, or absurdity, in the whole of literature" (172). Anthony Burgess: "He thought of words not as neutral rational counters, but as confetti, bonbons, artillery" (253). Roy Hattersley: "Overstatement was one of Chesterton's greatest pleasures" (368). Some writers marvel at his lack of restraint. Theodore Maynard: "Perhaps he should have curbed himself more than he did; but who except Chesterton had such an over-abundance that it needed to be curbed?" (50). Others simply think that he really is too much. Benny Green: "The attempt to read one of his books from cover to cover soon induces a kind of exhaustion...The quality which Chesterton seemed to lack utterly was stylistic restraint" (343). Bernard Levin: "An exaggerated style, like a garden in which everything is allowed to grow as it will, soon fades and rots" (178). John Gross: "He sees the world in terms of loud contrasts and garish colors; the picture has the boldness of a cartoon, but it lacks light and shade" (260). Malcom Muggeridge warns that responses to Chesterton are themselves frequently forced to be hyperbolic: "G. K. Chesterton is one of those writers for whom either too much or too little is usually claimed" (225).

7. *Collected Works*, vol. 16, 96.

8. Ibid., 45.

9. Ibid., 97.

10. Ibid., 329.

11. *A Half Century of Views*, 47. H. Marshall McLuhan also comments on this aspect of his prose: "Chesterton himself is full of that child-like surprise and enjoyment which a sophisticated age supposes to be able to exist only in children" (2).

12. Hugh Kenner makes this point perfectly: "He is not inventing illustrations, he is perceiving them." From *A Half Century of Views*, 88.

13. From *Collected Works*, vol. 16, 327–28.

14. Ibid., 328.

15. Ibid., 329.

16. To the wonderfully hyperbolic saying, often repeated in the light of the uncanny theories of modern science, that reality is not only stranger than we imagine but stranger than we can possibly imagine, Chesterton would retort yes, but it is not stranger than what we can see.

17. G. K. Chesterton, *Charles Dickens, A Critical Study* (New

York: Dodd Mead, 1913), 18. Page numbers from further quotations will be included in the text.

18. His book on *Robert Browning* (New York: MacMillan, 1904), could also be analyzed in this same fashion. The following comments about Browning apply equally, or even better, to Chesterton himself: "His intellect went upon bewildering voyages, but his soul walked in a straight road. He piled up the fantastic towers of his imagination until they eclipsed the planets; but the plan of the foundation on which he built was always the plan of an honest English house in Camberwell" (9–10). In other words, Browning's extravagance was in actuality perfectly proportioned to life itself. In fact, Browning also shares Chesterton's fundamental optimism: "Now the supreme value of Browning as an optimist lies in this...that beyond all his conclusions, and deeper than all his arguments, he was passionately interested in and in love with existence" (186).

19. For a sympathetic treatment of Chesterton's politics and his role in the movement known as distributism, as well as an analysis of Chesterton's occasional anti-Semitism, see Margaret Canovan, *G. K. Chesterton, Radical Populist* (New York: Harcourt Brace Jovanovich, 1977).

20. G. K. Chesterton, *St. Francis of Assisi* (New York: Doubleday, 1957), 22. He is talking at this point about the crusades. Page numbers of further quotations will be included in the text.

21. In discussing the troubadours, Chesterton notes the dangers of exaggeration: "There were manifest dangers in all this superb sentimentalism; but it is a mistake to suppose that its only danger of exaggeration was in the direction of sensualism. There was a strain in the southern romance that was actually an excess of spirituality..." (67).

22. The book, which appeared in 1905, defends Christianity only by negating the contrary. It is a defense of dogma in general, of common sense and moral accountability.

23. "Men will not believe because they will not broaden their minds" (24–25).

24. G. K. Chesterton, *Saint Thomas Aquinas* (New York: Doubleday, 1956), 23. All further page numbers will be included in the text. Chesterton's prose here is more restrained than in the earlier work, as befits his subject matter; but there is also a general shift in his style on which I will comment later in this chapter.

25. In a way, Chesterton's stylistic shift between these two works reflects, in a less dramatic fashion, the tempering of Karl Barth's prose between *Romans* and the *Church Dogmatics*.

26. G. K. Chesterton, *Orthodoxy* (New York: Doubleday, 1936). All page numbers will be included in the text. Note that at this point in his life Chesterton has not joined the Roman Catholic Church; that is still years in the future. By Orthodoxy he means the Apostles' Creed, or more vaguely still, traditional Christianity.

27. Given all the recent interest by theologians in narrative, Chesterton seems to be quite original in connecting religion and literature. In fact, he thinks Christianity affirms the dreams and hopes and answers the concerns and fears expressed in popular literature. "There is a great deal of real similarity between popular fiction and the religion of the Western people" (136). More generally speaking, "To a Christian existence is a story, which may end up in any way" (136).

28. On the denial of original sin, Chesterton is quite funny: "If it be true (as it certainly is) that a man can feel exquisite happiness in skinning a cat, then the religious philosopher can only draw one of two deductions. He must either deny the existence of God, as all atheists do; or he must deny the present union between God and man, as all Christians do. The new theologians seem to deny the cat" (15). On miracles, he is a bit flippant: "Reform or (in the only tolerable sense) progress means simply the gradual control of matter by mind. A miracle simply means the swift control of matter by mind" (127).

29. G. K. Chesterton, *The Everlasting Man*, from *Collected Works*, vol. 2. Pages numbers will be included in the text.

30. Notice how clear Ralph Waldo Emerson is, by comparison, on the relationship between Jesus and hyperbole. He argues that historical Christianity has repressed the radical message of Jesus and instead "dwells, with noxious exaggeration about the *person* of Jesus." Interestingly, Emerson thinks the problem has to do with the excessive nature of Jesus' language: "The idioms of his language, and the figures of his rhetoric, have usurped the place of his truth; and churches are not built on his principles, but on his tropes." From the Harvard Divinity School address, *Selected Writings of Ralph Waldo Emerson*, ed. William H. Gilman (New York: New American Libary, 1965), 246. Emerson argues that Jesus expresses what every person feels, what everyone can attain with their own effort. Jesus' extravagant language has, mistakenly, focused attention on his person rather than his message. Although Emerson claims to be doing justice to the poetry of Jesus, he reduces his message to that which goes without saying because we already know it. Indeed, there is a strong North American tradition of treating both Jesus' excessive teachings and the excessive claims about his divinity in

pragmatic terms. Note, for example, Thomas Jefferson's purified version of the New Testament and Benjamin Franklin's comment, "I see no harm, however, in its [the incarnation] being believed, if that belief has the good consequence, as probably it has, of making his doctrines more respected and better observed." Carl Van Doren, ed., *Benjamin Franklin's Autobiographical Writings* (New York: Viking Press, 1945), 784. I will return to the question of the extravagance of the incarnation in the last chapter.

31. *Orthodoxy*, 159–60.

32. *St. Thomas Aquinas*, 24.

33. Chesterton would concur with Teresa of Avila's sentiment that in religion hyperboles are only apparently so: "The things of the soul must always be considered as plentiful, spacious, and large; to do so is not an exaggeration." From *The Interior Castle,* trans. Kieran Kavanaugh and Otilio Rodriguez (New York: Paulist Press, 1979), 42. The poetry of excess is, to the saint anyway, the literalism of prose.

34. For a wonderful reading of chaos as a religious symbol, see Frederick J. Ruf, *The Creation of Chaos, William James and the Stylistic Making of a Disorderly World* (Albany: SUNY Press, 1991).

Chapter 6.

1. For a survey of various interpretations of this parable, and a reading of the story as an announcement of universal and unconditional salvation (both sons are, after all, accepted by their father), see Bernard Brandon Scott, *Hear Then the Parable* (Minneapolis: Fortress Press, 1989), 99–125.

2. Ibid., 116.

3. Ludwig Wittgenstein, *Philosophical Investigations*, trans. G. E. M. Anscombe (Oxford: Basil Blackwell, 1978), 19.

4. D. C. Muecke, *The Compass of Irony* (London: Methuen, 1969), 10. For a review of theories of irony, see my *Re-Figuring Theology, The Rhetoric of Karl Barth* (Albany: SUNY Press, 1991), chapter 5. In that book I trace irony's popularity to Kierkegaard, while I interpret Nietzsche as more representative of hyperbole. It is a more common procedure to interpret Nietzsche as one of the first fully ironic thinkers, but the textual evidence is ambiguous, at least from his middle period in which he praises the cool reflection of science as opposed to both the excesses of art and religion and the

irony of a culturally exhausted cynicism. Note this interesting comment about the excess of irony: "With regard to *origin, everything* human deserves ironic reflection: that is why there is such an *excess* of irony in the world." *Human, All Too Human*, trans. Marion Faber and Stephen Lehmann (Lincoln: University of Nebraska Press, 1984), 155 (aphorism 252). Nietzsche does not find this excess praiseworthy: "All ironic writers are counting on that silly category of men who want to feel, along with the author, superior to all other men, and regard the author as the spokesman for their arrogance. Incidentally, the habit of irony, like that of sarcasm, ruins the character; eventually it lends the quality of a gloating superiority; finally, one is like a snapping dog, who, besides biting, has also learned to laugh" (190–91, aphorism 372).

5. Jacques Derrida, "Cogito and the History of Madness," *Writing and Difference*, trans. Alan Bass (Chicago: University of Chicago Press, 1978), 61–62.

6. For an excellent analysis of how philosophy's unbalanced search for foundations created the problem of atheism, see Michael J. Buckley, S.J., *At the Origins of Modern Atheism* (New Haven: Yale University Press, 1987).

7. I should note that Rorty's polemical and sarcastic style is not limited to discussions of religion, but it is interesting that he rarely, if ever, talks about religion in any other way. For representative comments about religion, see *Consequences of Pragmatism* (Minneapolis: University of Minnesota Press, 1982), where he wishfully insists that theology has faded away from the cultural scene (xxii) and cannot be taken seriously in what he calls a postphilosophical culture (21 and 33–34). In *Essays on Heidegger and Others* (Cambridge: Cambridge University Press, 1991), he clearly states his hopeful belief in a Deweyan kind of social progress in which "without falling back into a desire for holiness…we shall no longer turn to the philosophers for rescue as our ancestors turned to priests" (26). Although he rejects the idea that reason can be defined, he is certain that rationality, whatever it is, precludes religious belief, and an increase in education will lead to a decrease in religion (a belief that has been empirically disproved). Besides this Victorian belief in rational progress, Rorty also puts religion in its place by stubbornly dividing private needs and beliefs from the public realm. The latter should be ruled by irony, and the former should be carefully contained so that private fancies do not get out of hand and upset the precarious but necessary achievement of liberal balance and moderation. For this compartmentalization, see *Contingency, Irony and Solidarity* (Cambridge: Cambridge University Press, 1989).

8. Although politics is the art of the possible and thus the crossroad of compromise, an excessive concern with civility and moderation can be one of the main stumbling blocks for social change. William H. Chafe, in *Civilities and Civil Rights* (New York: Oxford University Press, 1980), shows how white progressives supposedly supporting civil rights in Greensboro, North Carolina, were victims of their own shrewdness of civility. Their politics of moderation effectively enforced and sanctioned the status quo and subtly stifled social change in the guise of a benevolent paternalism. Chafe's analysis, of course, has wide ramifications. "Civility is the cornerstone of the progressive mystique, signifying courtesy, concern about an associate's family, children, and health, a personal grace that smooths contact with strangers and obscures conflict with foes. Civility was what white progressivism was all about—a way of dealing with people and problems that made good manners more important than substantial action. Significantly, civility encompassed all of the other themes of the progressive mystique—abhorrence of personal conflict, courtesy toward new ideals, and a generosity toward those less fortunate than oneself" (8). The relationship between hyperbole and politics is obviously complex. Although I agree with Chafe's analysis of civility, I tend to think that too often hyperbole is used in political contexts to denounce opponents from a position of self-righteousness. Religion represents the possibility of the impossible, the unlikely and yet necessary, in such a way that no individual can claim a privileged position or status. The best hyperboles of religion are both charged and inclusive, demanding and humble at the same time. For an excellent collection of essays on the lack of and the need for civility in a pluralistic culture, see Robert N. Bellah and Frederick E. Greenspahn, *Uncivil Religion, Interreligious Hostility in America* (New York: Crossroad, 1987). In his conclusion to this volume, Bellah refers to Richard Merelman's argument that the basic conflict in our culture lies between tight- and loose-boundedness (see Richard Merelman, *Making Something of Ourselves*, [Berkeley: University of California Press, 1984]). I agree with Bellah that the real danger is with the triumph of a loosely bounded culture: "There is a fear in our loose-bounded culture that strong belief in anything, particularly in the area of right and wrong, means one wishes to coerce others into sharing one's view" (231). Forms of discourse are needed that are bound to the particularity of tradition and community, rooted in passion and vision, without being coercive and absolutist. For a comprehensive analysis of the politicization of religion in the United States since World War II, see Robert Wuthnow, *The Restructuring of American Religion* (Princeton: Princeton University Press, 1988).

9. Max Weber is the key figure for the analysis of the rational-

ization of culture that requires the diminishment of religion. Note the following famous passage from *Science as a Vocation*: "The fate of our times is characterized by rationalization and intellectualization and, above all, by the 'disenchantment of the world.' Precisely the ultimate and most sublime values have retreated from public life either into the transcendental realm of mystic life or into the brotherliness of direct and personal human relations. It is not accidental that our greatest art is intimate and not monumental, nor is it accidental that today only within the smallest and intimate circles, in personal human situations, in *pianissimo*, that something is pulsating that corresponds to the prophetic *pneuma*, which in former times swept through the great communities like a firebrand, welding them together." *From Max Weber*, trans. and ed. H. H. Gerth and C. Wright Mills (New York: Oxford University Press, 1946), 155. Weber's response to modernity is a stoic acceptance of the negative consequences that follow from a minimalistic conception—as opposed to the fortissimo of hyperbole—of the self. He thinks that the only alternative to bearing "the fate of the times like a man" (155) is a nostalgic and regressive return to a magical and infantile relationship with the world. Like Freud and Bataille, he equates excess with a complete loss of the self identical to the infant's dependence on the mother. Reenchantment can occur only at the cost of a masculine independence and autonomy.

10. John Murray Cuddihy, *No Offense: Civil Religion and Protestant Taste* (New York: Seabury Press, 1978), 16. There are other rhetorical strategies of personalizing and thus privatizing excessive experiences and claims. Notice how the phrase, "Believe it or not..." begins a statement that is protected from public scrutiny and deprived of public impact by shifting the truth claim to a subjective response. The speaker abdicates responsibility for her or his own discourse.

11. Cuddihy connects this charge to forces internal to religion itelf; Protestantism has prepared for its own demise: "It is this taste, this Puritan plain decorum which has captivated us and which our culture knows as the most 'modern' and best good taste. This ineloquence, this understated esthetic of litotes, this decorum of imperfection, is the secular esthetic expressive symbol of the dissenting 'Protestant' (i.e., anti-Anglican, anti-Catholic) religious values of the Puritant origins of American identity. I call it, alluding to Max Weber, the Protestant esthetic" (192–3).

12. For an excellent overview of the historical foundations for criticisms of the theater, see Jonas Barish, *The Antitheatrical Prejudice* (Berkeley: University of California Press, 1981). Denys Arcand's recent film, *Jesus of Montreal*, suggests that the revival of both the

stage and religion must come in a common venture to find their common roots. In that film a group of actors renews its theatrical passion by reproducing the gospel story in all of its rawness and radicality; the corruption of both the church and the commercial entertainment industry combine to crush a spirit that is at one and the same time playful and pious.

13. Charles Taylor, *Sources of the Self, The Making of the Modern Identity* (Cambridge: Harvard University Press, 1989).

14. Paul Ricoeur, *The Symbolism of Evil*, trans. Emerson Buchanan (Boston: Beacon Press, 1969), 349.

15. This definition of the saint is from Edith Wyschogrod, *Saints and Postmodernism, Revisioning Moral Philosophy* (Chicago: University of Chicago Press, 1990), xxiv. Although I read this book only after I finished my own, I find its thesis congenial to my understanding of hyperbole. Wyschogrod does not explicitly discuss hyperbole, but she does connect morality to narratives of saintly or excessive desire. "The saintly desire for the Other is excessive and wild" (255). Only excess can mandate benevolence. "Saintly exertions have this effect because the extremism of saintly life compels attention" (243). I disagree with Wyschogrod, however, in her attempt to de-historicize and de-contextualize saints by disconnecting them from their theologies and religious beliefs. For example, she explicitly rejects any connection between saints and mysticism (see 38). The result is an articulation of excess that is, in spite of the retrieval of narrative and moral example, thin, vague and abstract. She never meets her own goal of showing how postmodernity can promote a concrete, particular morality by encouraging and valuing excessive acts of compassion and self-sacrifice. In spite of her acknowledgment that the Jewish and Christian traditions, in contrast to Nietzsche's rehabilitation of excess-as-ecstasy-for-its-own-sake, promote excess in terms of the priority of the Other, she disconnects excess from religion, rendering it idiosyncratic and idealistic. Unless saints-understood-as-figures-of-excess are seen as connected to particular communities and sustained by ultimate beliefs they will continue to be dismissed as, at best, marginal and powerless afterthoughts to the project of postmodernity. For a sympathetic critique of saintly excess, see William James, *The Varieties of Religious Experience* (New York: The New American Library, 1958), 264–85. For an account of saintly behavior toward Jews in a French Huguenot village during World War II made possible by a long tradition of pacifism and suffering, see Philip Hallie, *Lest Innocent Blood Be Shed* (NY: Harper, 1979).

16. Most of my comments about Weil have been influenced by the wonderfully hagiographical account in Simone Petrement,

Simone Weil, A Life, trans. Raymond Rosenthal (New York: Pantheon Books, 1976). This book is full of appropriate hyperbole about Weil: "Confronted by so pure a life, one hesitates to speak of it out of a fear of not being able to present it without changing it in terms of one's own inadequacies" (viii). She quotes one friend as commenting on Weil's search for purity that, "I doubt that anyone has ever pushed so far the respect for the superior part of oneself" (178). This inflexible self-concern could strike some people as arrogant and strident. Weil's self-concern, however, was always subordinated to a desire for sacrifice. In *Notebook V* she records a terrible prayer: "Father, in the name of Christ, grant me this. That I may be unable to will any bodily movement, or even any attempt at movement, like a total paralytic. That I may be incapable of receiving any sensation...That I may be unable to make the slightest connection between two thoughts" (quoted in Petrement, 486). Petrement frames Weil's death, which one newspaper headline termed "A Curious Sacrifice," as the climax of her extravagance: It "was not directly useful and was not an action, an intervention, but a refusal, an insistence on purity and loyalty to oneself" (36). Even the Marxist David McLellan, in *Utopian Pessimist, the Life and Thought of Simone Weil* (New York: Poseidon Press, 1990), is forced to recognize the unclassifiable excess of her life. He claims she is more like Tolstoy than St. John of the Cross, a French version of Kafka or a mixture of Pascal and Orwell. In the end, she is "the patron saint of all outsiders" (269). "If Weil imposed an abnormally harsh life upon herself, it was not because she was in love with suffering, but because, she felt, the suffering would enable her to love" (270). Moreover, in explaining her eccentricities, he writes, "With her vertigo of the absolute, it is not surprising that she sometimes found it difficult to keep her balance on the ground" (272). In her letters, Flannery O'Connor frequently mentions Weil, as in this fascinating passage: "The life of this remarkable woman still intrigues me while much of what she writes, naturally, is ridiculous to me. Her life is almost a perfect blending of the Comic and the Terrible...What is more comic and terrible than the angular intellectual proud woman approaching God inch by inch with ground teeth?" From Sally Fitzgerald, ed., *The Habit of Being* (New York: Farrar, Straus, and Girous, 1979), 105–6. There is also this revealing comment: "I think myself that Simone Weil is a trifle monstrous, but the kind of monstrosity that interests me" (*Habit of Being*, 522). Note the following for an example of Weil's sometimes outrageous comments: "Every time I think of the crucifixion of Christ I commit the sin of envy." From *Waiting for God*, trans. Emma Craufurd (San Francisco: Harper and Row, 1951). One of the most interesting treatments of Weil as a great hyperbolist, an essay that is basically a condemnation of hyperbole itself, is Susan Sontag's "Simone Weil," in *Against Interpretation* (New York: Dell, 1961).

17. Dietrich Bonhoeffer, *The Cost of Discipleship*, trans. R. H. Fuller and Irmgard Booth (New York: Macmillan, 1959). Page numbers will be included in the text.

18. In one of his last letters from prison, Bonhoeffer ambiguously retracts the heroism of *The Cost of Discipleship*, arguing that the Christian should be simply human, not holy and otherworldly. In my own terms, he was grasping for a Christian hyperbole that would lead toward this world, and not away from it: "I thought I could acquire faith by trying to live a holy life, or something like it. I suppose I wrote *The Cost of Discipleship* as the end of that path. Today I can see the dangers of that book, though I still stand by what I wrote. I discovered later, and I'm still discovering right up to this moment, that it is only by living completely in this world that one learns to have faith" *Letters and Papers from Prison*, ed. Eberhard Bethge (New York: Macmillan, 1972), 369.

19. Kenneth Burke, *The Rhetoric of Religion, Studies in Logology* (Boston: Beacon Press, 1961), 25.

20. Ibid., 8.

21. David Tracy, *Dialogue with the Other, the Inter-Religious Dialogue* (Louvain: Peeters Press, 1990). See chapters 1 and 5. This book constitutes a significant expansion of—or departure from?— Tracy's much celebrated analogical imagination in its dependence on excess language to describe the religious quest. Hyperbole replaces analogy. Note Tracy's enigmatic comment about the mystical-prophetic: "The hyphen is what compels my interest" (6).

22. See Ricoeur, *The Symbolism of Evil*, 352.

23. Søren Kierkegaard, *Attack Upon Christendom*, in *A Kierkegaard Anthology*, ed. Robert Bretall (New York: Modern Library, 1946), 468.

24. David Tracy's argument in *Blessed Rage for Order* (New York: The Seabury Press, 1975) is more metaphysical than my own, but I have learned much from this book. In it he begins with an existential analysis of basic human situations and moves toward an analysis of the kinds of language that respond to those situations. I prefer to begin with language itself, and find therein the signs of transgression and disorientation that comprise religious experience. Note his then-typical moves in the following quotes: "For that basic dimension to our lives a language re-presentative of the basic faith disclosed in moments of crisis and of ecstasy seems appropriate. That basic faith in the worthwhileness of existence, in the final graciousness of our lives even in the midst of absurdity, may be

named the religious dimension of existence" (119). Indeed: "One lives authentically insofar as one continues to allow oneself an expanding horizon" (96). The New Testament represents this horizon: "That intensification of ordinary proverbial language by the linguistic strategies of paradox and hyperbole alerts one to the limit of the ordinary use of such language and thereby discloses the properly limit-sense of New Testament proverbs. Its sense is the sense of all authentically religious language: the strange, jarring, paradoxical, and unnerving sense of a limit-language beyond the morality of traditional proverbial wisdom into the limit-domain of authentically religious speech" (125). "Literalize that language and that super-everyday world of supernaturalism called fundamentalism emerges" (126). Since *Blessed Rage*, Tracy has become more concerned with the primacy of language and less optimistic about the abilities of metaphysics. My own belief is that hyperbolic language can be grasped and understood, but I have no desire to ground it in some basic definition of authenticity or existence. Hyperbole, I suspect, speaks for itself.

Index of Names